*A transformational life journey to
awaken, empower and inspire*

Moira Darling

**SOL-BREK
BOOKS**

Published in 2016 by Sol-Brek Books

Copyright © 2016 Moira Darling

ISBN Paperback: 978-0-9955274-1-6
ebook: 978-0-9955274-0-9

A CIP catalogue copy of this book
can be found in the British Library.

Published with the help of Indie Authors World

IndieAuthors
World

Dedicated to Christine

To Michelle
With love fo
your amazy
futene life
adventires
Moira ♡

Acknowledgements

With heartfelt thanks to everyone who supported me on the journey to creating my book 'Sunshine in Neverland'. I have extreme gratitude to all the people who shared my life and in the process helped me build the strength to become a clearer, wiser and happier person. All the important relationships I experienced over the years showed me aspects of myself that I needed to access, or see about myself that were crucial to my growth. They brought me to understand that our most important priority is to have a healthy, loving balanced relationship with ourselves before we can truly share this with another person and that each challenge we face is an opportunity to strengthen and show us more of ourselves. Special thanks to Gail Connolly, Denise Ballantyne, Sue Hudd, Swati Hegde, Karen Darke, Anne Möeller, Nicky Darling, Joan Reddigan for your incredible individual input, help and unconditional love and support.

To Kim and Sinclair Macleod from Indie Authors World for their exceptional service, guidance, care and attention to detail I am eternally grateful.

Preface

This is the story of Moira's own personal journey into consciousness and leads us through the step-by-step, transformational process. This book came through as unexpected guidance when Moira cleared her life of everything that was interfering with her continuation to grow in consciousness and ability to step into true self-love. The space she created allowed a deeper and stronger connection to innate wisdom and intelligence to come forward and develop. Her trust in the guidance she receives is unquestionable. Her ability to listen without judgement, fear or trying to rationalize anything is essential to her work and life, as she has learned when she doesn't listen to the guidance her life becomes difficult and even chaotic. Her natural gift of insight is astonishing even to her, and difficult to explain or easy to understand intellectually. It is however simple, easy relatable and a clear connection to spirituality in a no nonsense, grounded and down to earth way.

While reading this book, reflect on your own life journey and connect with your own experiences that may have emotional similarities. Allow your interpretation to naturally flow allowing other perspectives to develop. Open to expand your self-awareness to one of greater compassion and kindness for your own life challenges, deepening unconditional love for yourself and your life.

We can read self-help books, meditate, talk about awareness and the meaning of life, endlessly searching for answers as we attempt to heal separation and fragmentation in our lives. But by simply acknowledging truthfully our own unique experiences and letting go of painful judgemental stories, we can strengthen our individual inner power and a deeper connection to Universal intelligence is able to transpire, bringing to us more overall clarity, wholeness, healing and peace.

Moira Darling

Chapter 1
The Beginning

October 4th 1999 was the day it happened, the turning point in my life. On that day I stepped onto a whole new path, and was taken in an entirely different direction from the well-trodden road I knew, far away from everything that was my 'normal'. It was a life-altering day when everything turned upside down, and profound changes began to spontaneously unravel themselves. I was unaware of the magnitude of what was about to happen and completely oblivious to the impact it would have on me. This day was the starting point to a journey of self-discovery and personal transformation taking me to heaven and through hell many times. I was to discover and experience the depths of emotional pain and pleasure, mental confusion, crystal clarity, chaos and peace, as the process of unlearning old beliefs, rediscovering and re-connecting to deeper truth began. It was the day I began to truly awaken.

Up until that day, I felt like an insignificant hamster running around in circles, only going through the motions, lost, getting nowhere, merely existing but not living, wondering what life was all about. I had no idea that the life-changing journey I was about to embark upon would bring me to a new depth of awareness. It was then that I realized that every new experience we have in our lives, whatever it is, comes with an opportunity to gain growth and insight on a deeper level beyond anything that we ever dared to imagine.

> Deep within the soul of each individual, treasures of wisdom reside patiently waiting to be discovered, connected with and set free. All of us, whoever we are, have the ability to reach a place of deep inner peace, truth and love. As each one of us courageously embarks on our own inner journey, re-evaluating our priorities and simplifying our lives, we come to appreciate what is most meaningful to us. This allows us to transform our fears, old limitations, conditioned beliefs and mindsets, and opens the secret door to realise our true-life purpose. It brings us to understand and accept the deeper meaning of true compassion, and self-love.

*

That day I found myself in a Château de Vine in France at a business function with three of my work colleagues. The company I worked for along with others from our industry were involved in a charity fundraising rally. The task for each of the participating companies was to race from Dover to Monte Carlo in Monaco, raising money for charity en-route. The plan was to drive towards the South of France during the day, while in the evenings we would meet for dinner and continue to raise more funds. Although this was for a great cause, to be honest for me personally, it was an amusing work jolly, and a very welcome change from the normal humdrum life I was living at the time.

During the course of the enjoyable evening, with great hilarity and a definite over indulgence of the endlessly flowing champagne, laughing as we attempted to speak French actually, it was more like franglaise or in my case franglaise with a Scottish accent, and was probably very offensive to the lovely, patient French waiters. Without warning it happened suddenly, what could only be described as a magical moment. Our eyes met and locked. Time seemed to halt, becoming silent, stretching into what felt like infinity. Yikes! I dropped my eyes to the floor to catch my breath, slightly freaked out. A second later I raised my eyes towards his gaze. Then I felt a flicker of a smile cross my face. He seemed familiar somehow. There certainly appeared to be a strong connection between us, a knowing on a different level, but most significantly, there was recognition, as if we had met before. Looking across the table towards him it seemed there was a communication between souls.

Ooookaaaaayyyy who is this, I thought? Then crazy as it seems, as we had never met before, "It's him" I felt as if I knew him. A curious mixture of emotions engulfed me. Initially I felt slightly wobbled, then a wave of calmness came over me. This made zero sense at the time, but somehow I knew, my life was about to move in a whole new direction and things would never be the same again.

The following day we re-focused back to the task at hand - the second stage of the rally. We were the only all women team in the event and unfortunately on the second day, we became hopelessly lost and arrived almost an hour late for the evening gala dinner. It was the nineties and long before the luxury of navigation systems! Firstly, we couldn't find our way to our hotel and secondly we couldn't find the venue where the dinner was being held. As we pulled into the car park very late and more than a little stressed, we nervously and rather sheepishly entered the restaurant, hoping to slip in unnoticed to join the dinner party. No way did that happen! As we walked through the door a loud cheer erupted from the room as all the businessmen and celebrities stood up and applauded, taking great delight in playfully mocking these four helpless 'having a blonde day' females arriving an hour late. Quickly recovering from our embarrassment we began to work the crowd. Well we had to play the game didn't we? Continuing the role, we bowed to the applause, laughing and coyly explaining our lateness saying, "Sorry we were shopping and got lost!" Everyone enjoyed the harmless and entertaining banter, all of it good innocent fun. As we scanned the room to find a seat we were surprised then delighted to see him and his colleagues waving to us, calling out "Come over! We have saved you seats at our table." They had held them for an hour until we'd got there. We spent another evening together.

For the rest of the week we had dinner with these high-powered businessmen. It was all very comfortable and entertaining. They commented on how refreshing it was for them to have 'business dinners' that were not hard work and instead we were all having a great deal of fun, we laughed a huge amount with them as they did with us. During these dinners, I never sat next to him, but we were both very aware of each other. While we maintained a distance, there seemed to be a vibe like an invisible thread connecting us. We were always happy to see each other and really looked forward to the evening frivolities.

The Gala dinner on the last evening was being held in the very beautiful Hôtel de Paris in Monte Carlo. He made sure he sat next to me. I felt his determination to connect and initially became slightly nervous. We made small talk around the table then he spoke to me directly. He leaned towards me and in a quiet whisper said "This might seem weird, but I feel like I know you and I would be really disappointed if I didn't get to see you again." Without a second thought, I turned around to look at him, and with absolute certainty replied, "But you do know me and of course you will see me again." What the heck was coming out of my mouth? The words had just tumbled out of their own accord, completely naturally as if I had no control over what I was saying. Slightly surprised, we looked at each other, followed by a pregnant pause. We both smiled feeling the intensely powerful connection between us. What on earth was going on? Next, as if to solidify our discussion, he pulled out his business card and wrote his home phone number on the back of it. As he handed it over he asked me not to share it with anyone else, and to call him.

Okay now, things like this did not happen to me! Coming from a little town in Scotland, this was way different from my typical life experience. I was not exactly oozing with confidence. Actually I had more than a tad of insecurity and also a big old chunk of an inferiority complex, but from that moment, my world began to slowly but surely be turned upside down. I was definitely blown away. My head was spinning and of course I was majorly flattered! An intense desire consumed me to get to know this stranger, who curiously, at the same time was so familiar. However, he was definitely not my usual type. An intelligent, handsome, bearded, professional and successful businessman, he was extremely well groomed with a suave, sophisticated style. He wore an immaculately starched shirt and a tasteful well-chosen tie with matching kerchief. His tailored suit looked expensive, and his shoes scrupulously polished. However, I instinctively felt there was something much deeper and more interesting concealed beneath the 'suit' image being displayed to the world and it seemed I was being given the opportunity to find out what that was.

Seriously, on the surface he was not my type at all, but then what was that anyway? The men in my life normally had a much less polished style, more comfortable in jeans tee shirts and trainers, than slick tailored suits and shiny shoes.

*

Back in my hotel room that night, unable to sleep, my mind relentlessly whirled with confusing thoughts and conversations with no one but myself. This fatalistic meeting was 'something'. Certainly I needed to get a handle on what this 'something' was, and the only way I could see to do this was to talk with him. After thinking about this over and over, I decided to act for my own peace of mind. I picked up a pen and notepad by the phone in the hotel room, and wrote him a note. I knew I would sorely regret not following my gut feeling with this extremely potent connection, and so writing the note was my first step towards bringing more peace to the situation. At the same time, I was not attached to what he did with it.

> When in a quandary, a good question to ask is "What will I regret more? Doing something, or not doing it?"

Regret can be difficult to live with and will affect our future peace of mind. Using this question to guide an action helps to clarify our decisions, especially when in unusual or difficult circumstances.

Once the note was written and sealed into an envelope, I felt more peaceful and finally drifted off for a couple of hours sleep. Eventually morning arrived and I showered, dressed quickly, pulling on some casual white trouser and my black 'just do it' tee-shirt. With one final look at the envelope, I checked in with myself again, "Hmmm should I?" Absolutely, my gut was telling me to go for it; there was no question. Certain of my decision, I took the elevator up to his floor and slid the envelope under his door and let it go. The next step was up to him.

The note simply read, "Maybe it would be a good idea to have a chat? Would you like me to drive you to the airport to catch your flight?" Clear and to the point, it sounded confident. I wanted to find out if this was all in my imagination and if this was real for him too? No matter what the outcome was, or what he did with my suggestion, for me, it absolutely felt like the right thing to do.

If we are urged to say or do something, even if it is way outside our normal behaviour or comfort zone, by not following these instincts, we can live to regret it and our peace can be impacted for a long time to come. It is always easier to make decisions and take actions when not attached to the outcome or to the other person's opinion. In this way the decision is made for our own peace and becomes nothing really to do with the other person. Decisions like this are coming from a place of value for our own peace of mind. On the other hand, when we attach to a specific outcome this can immediately result in stress and anxiety building within us, creating the opposite of peace. Our attachment to the outcome causes the anxiety - not the decision. This in turn, can make us too afraid to act on what we know is right for us, and we can miss opportunities and experiences that can help us emotionally grow.

I had joined one of his colleagues for breakfast and while we were chatting about the events of the week, he sauntered into the restaurant and pulled up a chair at our table. We smiled at each other and made pleasantries about the excellent breakfast, neither of us mentioning the 'note' that had been slid under his door, both of us waiting until we were alone.

Eventually when his colleague left, he looked at me, smiled and quietly said, "I got your note." Then he revealed that he was surprised and had almost stepped on it, as I had slid it under the door at the same time as he was leaving the shower room. But he was also delighted with my offer, and agreed we should take the opportunity to chat on the way to the airport. So if I didn't mind driving him there, it would be great. He also suggested that we leave a little earlier and we could stop somewhere for tea or coffee. We agreed to meet half an hour later in the hotel car park, both of us with the same opinion that we wanted to explore this a little further. Excited, I sneaked away not telling any of my teammates where I was going – this felt powerfully intoxicating and scary at the same time. Oh my!

We met in the garage and headed for my car. Completely forgetting us women had been travelling for days with not much time to clean up after ourselves, I opened the car door and was shocked at the state of the vehicle. I was appalled. I gasped a short sharp inhale of breath - the car was a pigsty. Sweet papers, empty crisp bags, clothing, empty water bottles, socks, bras etc., were strewn everywhere. A shocking mess, the clutter had piled up during the drive, and now I was faced with a rubbish pit. Horrified, I began stuttering and blabbering, trying to apologize for the mess. "Oh my, I'm so sorry I don't usually live like this," I said, mortified at the state of the car. This guy was immaculately groomed, and instinctively I knew that any car he drove would be pristine. He saw my shameful expression and laughed as he picked up a plastic carrier bag proceeding to fill it with rubbish. "I don't believe you just said that," he replied, tossing the now full bag into a litterbin. "There, it's all good."

My next mini-panic followed immediately after the pigsty car episode. Suddenly it dawned on me that I didn't have the parking ticket to get out of the garage. My boss had it in her purse. Instantly flustered, my anxiety loudly spoke, "How will we get out?" Not wanting anyone to know where I was going, and whom I was going with, I wasn't about to ask my boss for the ticket. Now what? Always so very anxious about everything I was babbling and flapping around like a trapped hen. In general I was very insecure and I always felt guilty about something or another most of the time. I had been like this for most of my life really. He on the other hand, seemed completely unconcerned. For him it was no issue. He told me to drive up to the exit, then got out of the car and walked over to the booth where the parking attendant was sitting. After a brief discussion in fluent French, the barrier was lifted and a second later we drove out. "What did you say to him" I asked incredulously, knowing if I were dealing with this, the outcome would not have been quite so straightforward. "It's no big deal" He laughed. Hmmmm…I thought, maybe it's not a big deal for some people.

> With every obstacle that presents itself, although it may not always be obvious, there is always a solution. To find this, it is important to stop, take a breath and respond to the situation rather than react in panic. At that time I was more in the habit of panicking and like a trapped bird got stuck in the drama of most problems. When in panic it is hard to even consider the idea of a solution, far less find one, as fear drives everything and creates more of the same.

We drove off towards the airport, completely on our own for the first time since we had met; and strangely, it felt natural and comfortable. The urge to discover more about this fateful meeting was impossible to resist, and it felt like there was no choice but to follow it. The need to connect during this small window of opportunity was intensely potent. It seemed fate had somehow offered to bring us together on that crazy, unexpected and unusual fundraising event. He had only decided to join at the very last minute and my company had joined only the week before it was due to start. It seemed too much like a coincidence. This of course added to the magic and mystery of the whole thing. It felt like our meeting was destined, almost as if we had no ability to do anything else except to go with it. Now it appeared that we had both jumped on board the rollercoaster ride that was about to take off. Fasten your seat belts people; we are going for a crazy one! Little did I know how crazy it really was!

We stopped at a little café bar somewhere in Nice. We sat outside in the sunshine, ordered tea, chatted, and laughed a lot. He did most of the talking, but it was a comfortable and easy couple of hours. Then, he brought out his camera and asked if it was okay to take my picture. Whoa! A bit surprised I agreed, but this was not how I was used to being treated – a man wanting to take my picture. Wow, that's new!

The time passed quickly as we got to know each other a little bit more. Being one on one with a man was unfamiliar territory and I certainly wasn't used to someone being interested in and happy to be with me. Good grief, looking back at that time, I was so insecure. I would describe myself like a cabbage patch doll, very green, naïve and lacking in confidence.

All too soon it was time to go. He paid the bill and we headed to the airport. I began thinking about my drive back to Monaco, I was nervous about finding my way back to the hotel. Not wanting him to know this, I pretended, or acted is a better description, that I was confident when he asked if I knew the way. Truthfully, really I wasn't. Being on my own in a foreign country, not speaking the language, driving a British car on the 'other' side of a fast moving motorway was a daunting prospect. Hey, I was anxious, I'm human, but I pretended I was cool. Although I wasn't cool at all! I wasn't even close to clapping the dog of a person who was cool! It wouldn't have mattered how insecure I was. Nothing, and I mean nothing, would have stopped me from driving this man to the airport that morning. Nothing would have stopped me at all.

Once we were parked at the airport terminal drop off point. Then it was time to say goodbye. Spontaneously we hugged and I kissed him on the cheek whispering "See you soon". Then, I got into my car and drove off waving, as if I had known him my whole life instead of only a few short days. Weird! Normally I didn't do this sort of thing, hug or kiss relative strangers! It was unusual for me to be so forward, but this time it was the easiest thing in the world to do. It felt so natural and comfortable as if I had been doing it forever.

*

As I began my journey back to Monaco alone, my mind began to whirl.

My current relationship was not going too well, but we had been involved for nine years. In that time our situation had been up and down like a fiddlers elbow. Now we shared a house together. However the truth was, it really never felt like a home. Our situation had evolved over time into a familiar, but very unhealthy, bad habit - one we both knew wasn't good for us. We were in denial, and couldn't see how harmful it was and therefore weren't considering giving it up. Deep down though, we weren't happy, my personal emotional wellbeing was tragic, but it was my 'normal' and therefore was pretty safe in a sick and co-dependent way. He worked hard and to relax was in the habit of 'partaking in a light refreshment or two,' which was actually having a few beers, sometimes in unfathomable quantities. This was just our standard way of life. Knowing I wasn't happy in my relationship was not enough, because at that time I had no idea what to do about it, and even if it became clear what to do, I did not have the confidence to take the necessary steps to change the situation.

> Even when we know something is not right for us, it's important not to give ourselves a hard time if we have not taken the action steps to change it. What is important is to understand that knowing is only one component of the complete picture. Preferably we also build inner-strength, confidence and trust, creating more safety for ourselves as we step into change. Unfortunately pain is often the catalyst for life changes.

Being around heavy drinking had always been part of the life and culture I was brought up in and I really never thought too much about it. Certainly I had no other point of reference for anything else, it was just normal. As a baby, whisky was probably used in my bottle to make me sleep, and as a tiny, skinny fifteen year old, I was often the proud winner of the weekend beer drinking competitions held at parties, more often than not, beating big burly male rugby players hands down. Interestingly, being clear-headed while working as a part-time bartender my relationship with alcohol began to change. It was then that it really hit home how the overuse of alcohol can negatively affect people, as I witnessed intelligent, dressed up, happy people, transform over the course of a few hours, into lost and broken souls. Often it left them emotionally fragmented, unrecognizable from their conscious selves becoming disheveled, argumentative and occasionally incapable of speech. Not a pretty sight! Observing this common, acceptable form of self-harm was a bit of a wake-up call as far as my own drinking habits were concerned. Recognizing if I didn't like what was happening to other people when they drank heavily, it was highly unlikely I would like it in myself.

Why? Because, I could be just as big a fool as anyone else when alcohol was driving my bus. This information did not make me teetotal but thank goodness it gave me the ability to develop a healthy respect on how to use alcohol a lot more responsibly than I had previously done.

> It is sobering to experience and witness first hand, how heavy alcohol use has the ability to obliterate the dignity of an intelligent human being. It can demolish any level of self-awareness and it distorts our perception of reality. It often ruins self-esteem, can destroy loving relationships and friendships, brings uncertainty and fear into the lives of everyone involved, but even more horrifying is that people who are drunk can often feel and think they are clear and sober. Even if they are crawling across the floor on their hands and knees they truly believe they're okay, insisting they are 'fine'. Alcohol mixed with tension, stress and human pain, becomes a crazy chemical cocktail disguised as 'fun' erupting and exploding minds and bodies. Denial of reality affects both the drinker and the people close to them as the unpredictability, chaos and mental confusion becomes a normal way of life. Denial is used as a coping mechanism and can unfortunately trap us on the merry-go-round, going around in circles, never being able to leave Neverland.

As the wheels of my mind whirled with all sorts of crazy insights flooding over me, it became clear to me without doubt that change needed to happen, but first things first right now my job was to find my way back to Monaco. Gritting my teeth and with sheer determination, I navigated my way out of the airport and nervously pointed the car in what I hoped was the correct direction towards Monaco. I kept everything crossed and prayed I wouldn't cause chaos on the road, after all there was more than enough chaos going on in my head! Beads of sweat pushed their way onto my forehead as I arrived at the first pay toll. I scrambled in my handbag for change and thankfully found some, which I threw it into the bin and passed through, uneventfully. Hmmm not too bad after all! The second pay toll was even easier. Encouraged I continued on with my heart pounding and my mind full of whirling thoughts, then all of a sudden, there in front of me was the familiar square in Monaco. Incredibly I had made it back and had managed to do so without injuring or killing anyone. Also, importantly, the car was in one piece and so was I well physically anyway. Breathing a huge sigh of relief I gave myself a silent but very much appreciated pat on the back, as this was a proud moment. I had achieved something I thought I couldn't. Now I needed to find the hotel. After circling Monaco several times, I eventually found it. Relieved I drove into the entrance of the garage and parked the car.

> One of the most important things we can do for ourselves is to note the moments when we have done something that for us as individuals is a big deal. This helps to anchor in our abilities and helps us grow in confidence. What we have done may not be particularly significant to anyone else, but if we have pushed through our comfort zone, it is important for our self-esteem that we acknowledge ourselves.

My colleagues met me in the hotel foyer and greeted me with a zillion questions. "Where on earth have you been?" was the first of the barrage. They couldn't work out what had happened, especially when they saw that the car had gone. By this time I had been missing for several hours, with no communication as to my whereabouts. When I revealed where I'd been, it was difficult to decide what surprised them more - the fact that I had driven to Nice on my own, or I had taken him there. They were all, "What? You drove to Nice on your own. You dropped him at the airport? You found your way back here on your own?? Whoa, Brave you." Yes I agreed, I'm brave, very, very brave, but not for the reasons they were thinking.

My boss, who was quite insightful and worldly, looked at me with a glint in her eye and laughingly stated in her boss-like manner, "As your boss I have seniority and need you to step aside, I want him." I laughed, knowing she was only slightly joking, and given half a chance she would go for it. She was certainly attracted to him. Feigning a sad expression of apology I explained to her, "Sorry I can't! It's too late. It's a done deal. We have a connection going on that I don't under-stand at all, but what I do know is, it's something." Unlike her, I was not joking! It seemed I was being swept away on a tidal wave of emotion. My heart felt lighter than it had been in a long time. A new sensation, deep down in my belly was beginning to smoulder like a fire igniting new possibilities for my happiness. The potential building within my heart was incredibly seductive. Buckle up people; we're going for the ride of our lives but right now I needed to lie down, take a nap and breathe!

During the trip I had opened up a little about my life to my team. With only one mobile phone to use between us on the rally, I had just borrowed it to call home and check in with how things were going there, and to share some of my adventures. As usual the conversation was all about what he was dealing with, how he was, and the many sorry tales of one dreadful drama after the other, my activities were never even mentioned. After listening to yet another frustrated rant, followed by a subtle guilt trip being dropped on me, I hung up the phone and pleaded with the girls to help me. "If I ask for the phone again, please do not give it to me, I do not want to ring home." After each call, it felt as if a main artery had been slashed and I was hemorrhaging my vital energy. My heart was heavy as if someone was sitting on my chest, weighing me down, and it was exhausting. For the first time it became obvious how my energy was being impacted by negativity. Also, very importantly, I recognised that by asking the girls not to hand me the phone was a clear indication that I didn't feel strong enough to trust myself.

> Being in a vibration different from what we are accustomed to helps us to identify the difference and gives us a new point of reference for something that may be healthier for us. It is incredibly important to understand the effect of negative energy has on us over long periods of time. The constant stress will make our body tense up causing muscle and joint pain. It activates our sympathetic nervous system and stress hormones flood our bodies locking us into 'fight or flight' mode. This affects us in many ways, including our quality of sleep,

ability to rest, our digestive systems and blood pressure. It can cause us to develop many ailments that can be devastating for our wellness and overall health.

A new understanding had dawned on me and I was now asking myself questions I had never even considered before. Good grief, is this how my life is the whole time? The week of the rally had been one of the most wonderful, exciting, fun times of my life EVER. Although a unique situation and not 'real' life, it was an opportunity to experience the complete opposite vibration of energy than my normal. During the entire time I had had a taste of mutual respect, kindness, fun and appreciation. I had been acknowledged and was able to be myself without concern. Yes, I was still insecure and nervous but I was not tiptoeing on eggshells - I hadn't realised how much I did that. The week away from my 'normal' life had allowed me to see a new reality and how much serious denial I was in, living a lie, in an illusion. For the first time, I became aware of how unhealthy and unhappy my life truly was. More importantly now I understood the impact it was having on my mental, emotional, physical and spiritual wellbeing. By stepping back it became clearer about what was really going on. This trip was a new point of reference, it had shown me another way of relating with people, and fortunately I liked it, a lot.

When we are normalised to our environment and surrounding vibrations, it becomes difficult to identify how damaging these situations may be. Negativity, disregard and disrespect can then become okay for us. It is not until we step out of this norm that we can see the difference and experience another reality.

Now time to start the journey home, our team had opted to drive back together, stopping in Paris for one night before catching the channel ferry back to the UK. Away from our families and coming from very different backgrounds, we supported each other while confined in the car for days. No longer just work mates, we had become real friends, bonded by the lifetime of emotions we shared on this short but unforgettable expedition. Singing, laughing raunchily as we played jokes, we also argued, cried and hugged each other when needed.

Knowing we were coming to Paris for the night, he had kindly offered to meet, and take us out for dinner. He had gone out of his way and had also arranged a hotel for us. During our drive north, my boss communicated with him regarding these arrangements, openly flirting in the phone conversations. I observed, but kept out of it completely. I found this interesting, as normally that kind of thing would have intimidated me. It certainly would have increased the terrible inferiority complex and insecurity I had running at that time. But strangely it didn't bother me at all. Now deep in thought, having had a fair amount of inner dialogue with myself and wondered if I had imagined this whole thing. I could almost feel him. Our connection was so strong but at the same time I was not physically attracted to him. I knew very little about this man apart from the fact he loved all kinds of music, and like me, random songs with meaningful lyrics bringing insightful messages would sometimes play in his mind. Soul to soul, it was as if we had known each other for lifetimes, cut from the same cloth, or opposite sides of a coin.

Meeting a soul mate is an amazing gift. These connections are rare, profound and life changing, although not always in the way we would expect. Sometimes when a soul mate enters our lives, they shake us, wake us up and with unending love, will kick ass to move us into living the life we are meant to have and reach the potential we are destined for.

As we drove into Paris through the overwhelming traffic, the beautiful, vibrant city immediately enthralled me. Although it was my first visit to this incredible place, I offered to drive as none of the girls felt brave enough to manoeuver the busy streets. Parisians drive fast and I fitted in well! Quite literally, taking our lives in our hands, with every man for themselves, we spun around the Arc de Triomphe twice, in the ridiculously fast Parisian traffic! After losing our way many times, and with a great deal of swearing and squeals of terror from the back of the car, we eventually found our quaint little hotel which was hidden down one of the tiny narrow streets. We were exhausted so we checked in and took a well-earned nap. A couple of hours later, refreshed, we were ready to drink in the cosmopolitan atmosphere of the city, do some shopping and sightseeing before dinner. Could this day get any better? Apparently it could!

We arrived at the restaurant he had chosen. Beautiful, decorated with pictures of Buddha it had a calm, easy and peaceful, ambiance. I was unable to hide my astonishment and silently mouthed over to him, "Wow thank you! This is amazing!" The restaurant was right up my alley and embodied my interests perfectly. He remembered that we had talked about my appeal towards spirituality, consciousness, and personal development while we were in Nice. Though at that time it was more of a hobby than a way of life. My attraction was really based on my difficult life experiences and what I called 'my weirdness.' By this I meant, that since childhood I had always had the ability to see, predict, and have insights into things that were not always obvious or seen on a physical level. Without support or the ability to deal with it properly, it felt more like a curse than the gift as some saw it. This so-called "gift" caused me a lot of stress, anxiety and occasionally even pain. For this reason I shut it down for many years and had only recently begun to open up to this part of my life again. Now I was dabbling with spirituality but didn't truly apply it to my real life. It seemed unbelievable to me that he had deliberately chosen this fitting place. People going out of their way to give me something they knew I would enjoy was extremely unfamiliar territory, and to be honest I had no idea how to handle it. Very insecure and unsure of myself, my personal healing hadn't properly begun.

After a fabulous meal, we hit the town and headed to a cocktail bar in Le Bastille. There we ordered 'zombies' a colorful mixture of alcohol and fruit, appropriately named as the result after a couple of these babies, would leave us like the walking dead. One zombie more loosened us up even more than we already were, and the outrageous laughter was endless. It was a hilariously fun night but not crazy. At one point in the evening he put his hands around my waist and whispered in my ear, "Are you enjoying yourself?" Immensely flattered by the attention, I nodded and smiled, thinking of course, do you really need to ask?

The night was coming to an end, it was late and the temperature had dropped. I hadn't brought a coat with me and began to shiver with the cold. Noticing this, he took off his jacket and wrapped it around my shoulders. Big and comfortable, I felt cared for in the blanket of warmth. Then out of the blue we were unexpectedly caught in a brawl as a fight broke out in the street with some drunken youths. Suddenly a police van screeched to a halt right next to us and dozen or more French policemen tumbled out of the van and ran towards the fight. Within minutes and with great efficiency, they dragged the fighting boys roughly into the back of the vehicle. Quickly he put his arm out and gently ushered us into the night. "We don't want to be involved with the French police," he said calmly. My, oh my, it seemed as if this man knew how to deal with anything and everything. This not so streetwise, small town girl was awestruck and mesmerised.

Completely unconcerned about having had a drink earlier in the evening, he expertly drove his car through the busy streets of Paris until he pulled up outside our hotel. It felt weird to be saying goodbye. He hugged and thanked my two friends, then my boss. It was obvious that she liked him, making sure she sat next to him at dinner and in the passenger seat of the car. Fascinated by this whole experience I stayed in the background. He never encouraged her one bit, but he later told me she had whispered to him, "Call me." He didn't! Next he hugged me a little too long not to notice. I kissed him lightly on the cheek and quietly whispered in his ear, "I'll call you soon." He smiled saying, "Good, I hope so." Then he drove off into the night leaving us standing in the now quiet, dark street of Paris wide eyed and slightly stunned. In unison we gasped, "Wow! What a night! Oh man! It was priceless." The fantastic evening was a truly wonderful ending to our amazing trip, but now as we slipped silently into our quaint little Parisian hotel, it was time to fall into a contented and happy sleep.

Feeling slightly sad, the next day we caught the ferry back to the UK and another reality. With my team safely dropped home to their delighted families, I looked forward to having some quiet time on the eight-hour journey back to Scotland as I needed to go over the events of the previous few days in my heart and mind. It felt unexpectedly strange to be going back to a lifestyle that only a few days prior was all I knew. The entire trip had been incredible, and one of the most amazing and magical times of my entire life. I felt empowered and stronger than ever, but more especially I was happy and this was an utterly new feeling for me. Dangerously over thinking I began to wonder if it had all been a surreal dream. Did all these experiences really happen, or had the whole trip been in my imagination? But I was unable to deny how strong and confident I felt. What had happened was to profoundly change the course of my life, but what, when and how these changes were to manifest was yet to unfold. Now my next step was to pay attention and listen to the best of my ability. If my life was to change and never be the same again, it was not time yet!

> **Listening and paying attention is the opposite of going through the motions, in denial and habitually repeating the same old, same old behaviour patterns. Our soul wisdom is an inner knowing that can sense life changes long before they manifest in the physical reality. Listening to this wisdom we learn patience and how**

to recognize the signs all around us, guiding us through
the steps towards creating a new life.

*

Now driving up the single-track road leading to my home and
into my 'real' life, a different greeting awaited me than any I
had experienced during the previous week. My work 'jolly'
was over, and a lot was waiting to be taken care of at home.
Going through the door I plummeted headfirst into the
barrage of waiting needs. My trip never mentioned, erased as
if it hadn't happened, the gifts of lovely French wine brought
back from some of the villages we had visited en–route
ignored, but waiting impatiently for attention was the restaurant, laundry, cleaning, people, everything was awaiting my
return. This palpable lack of acknowledgment or appreciation
stood out to me like a sore thumb, but that's just how it was.
I sensed a tad of resentment had brewed over me wasting
time "gallivanting in France" when so many more important
things were here - waiting!

Probably for the first time none of this bothered me. Still
happy and nourished from the energy of my trip, I didn't
care! Interestingly I had gained some immunity to the judgment, negativity, pressure and criticism that was incessantly
around me at home. Being out of this environment with very
little contact for almost two weeks, I was revitalized and had
a new point of reference. During my time away, experiencing
the opposite energy, it became strikingly obvious to me how
unhealthy the life I lived actually was. Clearly this was a bit
of an epiphany, and I decided to pay much more attention.
Possibly there was another way to live? Maybe there was such
a thing as being happy?

It is not easy to identify circumstances and situations that may be unhealthy for us while we are immersed in them. By stepping back from these lifestyles and giving ourselves another point of reference, we can see more clearly our reality. This in turn helps us to make better, healthier choices for our lives. Until we awaken and see the difference, we are unaware of the choices we have and therefore can make.

Up until the time, I had never felt truly happy, in fact I believed some cosmic mistake had occurred and landed me in the wrong place by accident. Life simply felt too hard! There was a firm belief running in my mind I would die young, and that my life would end when I was 47. For the first time in my life I was feeling somewhat different obviously this was really important. Throughout my life I had always felt deep sadness. Now I felt a warm vital light nourishing my heart, radiating through to my soul that can only be described as sunshine. This was a new experience and like a starving bird I wanted more. In fact the truth was I desperately needed a lot more.

As I unpacked my bag from the trip, I realized a pair of my sandals had been left behind at the quaint little hotel in Paris. A call to the hotel confirmed this. Hmm should I ask him to pick them up for me? Nope I didn't think so. I wasn't about to put him out of his way, plus I was too shy to ask him, so for the time being I let them go.

As people pleasers we don't like to ask for help and are very uncomfortable with the idea of putting anyone out of their way, preferring to suffer in silence. On the other hand, we are the first to jump in, offering help to anyone and everyone, even those who don't want or need it. This creates a serious imbalance in our lives and reduces our self-value, as the only way we feel important is by helping others. We become martyrs to the needs and lives of everyone else, including passing strangers and stray dogs. We genuinely do care for others and our intentions are well meaning, but underneath is our own unconscious need to be needed, to feel significant and more importantly to feel love. This stems from low self-esteem, judgement and it gives us a sense of importance and control.

*

A few days later, back at work on the road as a sales rep, stressed and irritated, hopelessly lost and running late for my appointment with a new customer, my car phone rang. His call was unexpected. I was flattered to hear his voice and I noticed my mood change immediately, instantly I felt happier. He asked me how my trip home was and how I was doing? It was hard to pretend. Having been back in reality for a few days, I had come down to earth with a shuddering bang. Already, I had begun to re-absorb the old vibe that was normal for me, i.e. stress, pressure, sadness and hard, hard work – I had no time for myself at all. I know he sensed my disinterest in discussing how I was doing as I swiftly changed the subject to my preoccupation with finding my customer. Nevertheless, I now couldn't deny that he appeared to be pursuing me.

Later, the following week, I called him back. It was around midday and he was just about to head out of his office for lunch. The tone of his voice communicated his delight that

I had called. We had a lighthearted conversation about the rally and our individual journeys home. When he told me his flight had been delayed in Nice a thought flashed through my mind, "I wish I'd known and we could have spent more time together." He asked me for my home address so he could mail me something. This surprised me, and to be honest, I felt it was a bit forward of him, but unable to bring myself to challenge this, I gave it to him. Then I mentioned my sandals left behind at the hotel, and he immediately insisted on picking them up for me. After a little back and forth banter, with me arguing it would be too much trouble, he continued to persist and reluctantly I agreed. A few days later to my surprise a letter arrived from him, saying he found it wonderful how we had met and would love us to meet again soon, either in France, Scotland or UK, and, get this, he looked forward to "hearing my observations." Enclosed was a card from the restaurant where we had had dinner on that special night in Paris. He thought I would like it. Actually I loved it. Oh my, I laughed! My sandals however, were still in Paris.

A few weeks later and after only one or two phone conversation he informed me he was coming to the UK for business, and could we meet? If this were possible, he would bring my sandals? Eeek! Panic stations, but hey, what was I going to do? Not go? I didn't think so! At the very least I had to check this out, and find out what the heck this was. Once I knew more, I could either let it go or let it grow. More especially for me it was important to see how I felt when we met again.

Deciding to meet was a no brainer. I booked a room in the hotel where he would be staying, and after the long drive, arrived at the hotel with my imagined, imaginary chastity belt securely fastened, padlocked, with an electric wired fence, safely in place. Once I was checked in and settled I sent him a message to let him know I was in the hotel. When we were making the arrangements, he asked me to tell him all about myself when we got together. This was a new phenomenon, a man interested in my story! Self-doubt and judgment taking over, I thought when I told him my stuff that'd be it, done. I never, ever talked about my life, blocked it out, hid it, ignored and forgot it – yes absolutely, but talk about it, never! Back then, shame and denial were in charge of my life. Okay, this was way outside my comfort zone, on as many levels as I could think of, but I thought I may as well get it over with, after all after he hears this lot I'd never see him again anyway. We ordered room service, I talked, and he listened. As I began to tell my sorry tale to this relative stranger, I had no idea that the vital lesson of listening, trusting and honouring myself was about to begin.

Whenever we stretch ourselves beyond our normal level of comfort we expand and grow. This applies on any aspect mentally, physically, spiritually or emotionally. To step outside of our emotional comfort zone is one way to build our emotional maturity and reduce self-judgement. It is often the more challenging as it involves feeling our emotional vulnerability, which is really uncomfortable but essential for our emotional intelligence to build.

Chapter 2
Before the Beginning

Right from the beginning my perspective on life seemed to be unusual, relative to the people around me. I was born and raised in an insular and traditional Scottish town and as a young child my favourite hang out was the local library, in an attempt to satisfy my fascination with books on art by the great masters and the fairy world. Sensitive as a child I was often overcome with a feeling that something was not quite right with the world. Fantasy appealed to me far more than the reality that surrounded me. Most of the people in the small town were factory workers, including my family. Although it probably wasn't the case, to relax, they seemed to have an endless flow of house parties one weekend after the other. Barrels of home-made beer were stored beneath the stairs, bottles of whisky always stocked up, some hidden at the beginning of the night as a backup supply in case they ran out. We would all pile into the old battered cars that my father proudly reconditioned to be driven to yet another party. Christmas and New Year were particularly busy times and a huge effort was made to attend as many houses as possible, drinking copiously throughout. One New Year my father's friend was driving an old ford car, taking us through the narrow lanes to a farmhouse in countryside, drunkenly singing 'Sailing up the Clyde'. The old car was overflowing with kids and some inebriated adults. I was sitting squashed up in the back seat feeling anxious and unsafe, thinking resentfully "I hate this – this is not happy and when we get to the party we have to say Happy New Year" I was anything but happy not wanting to be there at all but with little choice in the matter, I knew I had to just put up with it. Then I became aware the singing had abruptly stopped. Suddenly, all chaos broke out as the driver threw up all over the windscreen. Now unable to see the road, he made a futile attempt to clear the smelly, sticky mess away from the window by turning on the wiper blades! Unable to comprehend why this wasn't doing the trick as the problem was on the inside and not the outside, the screams of disgust and horror erupted from the back seat, adding to the ridiculousness of the situation. This little episode would be laughed and joked about later at the party, minimizing the danger and the disgust we children felt.

> Minimizing any situation is equally as damaging as over-dramatising. Denial of reality and lack of responsibility causes this to happen. It creates self-esteem issues and problems with confidence and trust, as it causes us to question if what we have experienced is our imagination or were we really in danger. However, we know we have had a significant experience that for us as individuals was uncomfortable and even scary. When these experiences are invalidated or dismissed due to insensitivity and lack of awareness caused by alcohol, we can become emotionally confused and insecure.

As a ten year old tomboy I loved hanging out with friends from my neighborhood, doing our favourite outdoor pastimes, riding our bikes, climbing trees and building wooden go-carts and dens. However, I always felt that something was not quite right with my world. One day struggling to make some sense of this and not being able to, I was listening to conversations my friends were having. We were playing on our bikes and had stopped for a break. A strange stillness suddenly came over me and a thought crept quietly but clearly into my mind. "I think differently from other people, and I know I can see things that other people don't see, I just wish I could have a moment in their minds because I know it is so different from what I experience." Not knowing what else to do with this insight, I just decided right then, I was weird.

My eyes transfixed me and I would spend hours looking in the mirror pushing up the outside corners, making them slightly slanted, recognizing a person from an entirely different culture from the one I was living in. Somehow I felt a mistake had happened and I had landed in this strange place with people who were not really living and had no understanding about life. When I was out with my friends, I imagined my family at home as skeletons, instead of living people. A skeleton would be sitting on an armchair watching TV, one would be washing the dishes with an apron on, and there was a baby skeleton lying in a baby crib. Although very young at the time, this didn't scare me at all. It was just how I saw things. My father had always called me a witch, of course this was not true, but from his perspective I was strangely peculiar. As a child I frequently dreamt that I could fly out of my bedroom window above the street, into forests and mountains. The experience of travelling through the night into different realms was incredible and felt freer and more natural than my normal waking world. But when my eyes opened after a night of soaring through the ethers in my dreams and I fell once more into the dense physical reality, my heart sank becoming tired and weary.

*

In primary school I played sports in a big way. Using any excuse to be outdoors, I played netball, hockey, rugby, swimming, running, cycling I loved it all. At the age of eight with the diagnosis of Type 1 diabetes, my love of sport increased and became my way of proving to everyone that I was 'normal' - at least physically.

The news shattered my parents, and understandably they found the situation very difficult. As they did with most uncomfortable things, it was handled by basically ignoring it, apart from playing the game at my clinic appointments. The day before my father took me for my six-monthly check-up, he filled out my journal of blood test results, then as a reward for getting through another stressful check up, we had 'High Tea' in a nice restaurant. Of course this was not the wisest way to respond to my appointments, but was how things were. It was never really talked about and no one made a big deal of it. In a way, for this I am thankful, as it never defined me as a childhood illness sometimes can.

> Often when we are given a label or a diagnosis, it is easy to become identified with it. In the process we become the patient with a label, and we lose our individuality as people. This can victimize us, and can take over

and define us. Then unfortunately it is easy to live your life becoming the label and fear then drives our every choice. Being afraid of the possible prognosis creates immense stress on our immune system, and does not support wellness. I chose at a very young age to not embody the label I was given. This is not the same as being irresponsible. It simply means I am a person first, who deals with my situation without fear, focusing on wellness rather than sickness.

Of course however, it actually was quite a big deal but no one at home was able to cope with it sensitively, and at school it was the same. The first Easter after my diagnosis, the teacher was handing out sweets to the entire class as a treat. Finally she approached my desk. Awkwardly her eyes avoided me as she said, "Oh, you can't have any because of your diabetes." Not knowing what to say or do I just looked down at my desk feeling my face instantly turning crimson with shame and embarrassment, the rest of the class all staring at me happily by now sucking on their sweets. Now of course she was right and this was true but her poor handling of the situation and the unintentional, insensitive delivery felt harsh, and was to impact me for many years to come. Being a sensitive nine year old, the feeling of exclusion was locked in and my interpretation there was something broken or wrong with me slipped into my psyche. I felt this intensely, but hiding it from the world, I begun to internalize, personalise and feel ashamed of my condition. At that time in the sixties diabetes was not as common as it is now, and I felt alone, stigmatised and self-conscious. I dealt with it by ignoring the problem and focusing on sports, now feeling like I had to prove to everyone that I was strong.

> An unkind or insensitive look or word from a teacher, parent or adult in authority can scar young hearts and minds so easily. If these traumas are not identified and healed they are carried forward into our adult lives.

Surprisingly, over forty years later an opportunity arose to heal this old emotional trauma. Looking for insurance coverage for our small company my business partner and I invited an insurance agent to our office to discuss our requirements. Obviously, given my health condition, we wondered if it was possible but after providing him with specific details, he assured us he could organise something. It was all very amicable, and we arranged to discuss his proposal the following week. From the beginning of our second meeting he focused his attention only on my partner and did not even look in my direction. Heavy anxiety began to bubble up in my belly as I listened to him, this was exacerbated as he continued to ignore and exclude me from the conversation as if I was not even in the room.

> We sometimes deal with uncomfortable situations by avoiding them entirely. This causes more discomfort for the people involved.

The precise emotional sensations I had felt all of those years ago in the classroom as a nine year old began to stir unexpectedly, then suddenly exploded within me. Thankfully by this time I was experienced and fairly skilled with emotional healing and without doubt connected that this unsuspecting man was giving me a golden opportunity to heal a deep childhood wound that I had been carrying for over forty years. Understanding this and now with new purpose, I continued to observe my process as he completely disregarded my presence, focusing only on my business partner.

I concentrated my attention on allowing the old pain I was holding to intensify in my body, mind and heart. After a few minutes, the energy had built enough for me to take action. Taking a deep breath I raised my hand to stop the conversation and get his attention. Although we had been together in the room for around fifteen minutes by this time, he appeared surprised to see me. I smiled and said "Hi!" forcing him to connect. The truth was, I really did not feel like smiling. Actually, part of me felt like ripping his head from his shoulders, as the anger at being ignored intensified. I had been triggered and my immediate reaction was to blame him for how I was feeling. Thankfully with a conscious understanding that this was my stuff, and nothing to do with him, I continued to smile - he was simply an unaware and unwitting participant who was helping me to heal an old wound from my past.

However, the energy was powerful and in an effort to maintain my composure I took a slow, deep breath before politely speaking, "I take it this proposal is for both of us?" He gave me a startled look, then he opened his mouth and almost verbatim I heard the exact same words my insensitive teacher had uttered to me all of these years ago: "Oh you can't have anything. There's nothing I can give you because of your diabetes." In that second it was as if a time capsule had jettisoned me back almost forty years to plop me down at my school desk once more. Of course now, I was no longer that little child, but, for forty years, buried deep within the cells of my body had lain the old unhealed trauma, emotionally locking me into that childhood moment. Now it was up, exposed, ready to be acknowledged and mended. What a gift!

As humans we naturally do what we can to avoid pain, emotional or otherwise. The energy can feel completely overwhelming when triggered. One way of dealing with this is to manage it, and try to avoid situations that may remind us, but if we can allow the pain to come instead of running away from it, we have an opportunity to heal. This has to be done wisely and with great awareness, as the powerful often painful or angry victim energy builds, we will have the urge to lash out and attack those who have initiated the hurt. It is our old pain, and by facing it rather than avoiding it, we can heal deep traumas, but this takes courage and presence.

Although ridiculously uncomfortable to revisit, I consciously allowed the old painful emotional energy to intensify even more in my body. I closed my eyes to centre myself, inhaling slowly and deeply, again and again. Gently piece by broken piece, the fragmentation that had occurred all those years ago began to connect and pull together into peaceful wholeness. Opening my eyes I looked straight at this guy who had no idea that he had offered me far more than any stupid insurance plan and courteously I said "Thank you for bringing your proposal, however, it seems you cannot provide us with what we asked for." He looked shocked and started to flap around a bit "Oh, I can maybe, blah! blah! blah!" He went on, stuttering explanations, but I was no longer listening to him. My business partner had picked up on what was happening and supported the process, as I continued taking charge of myself "Maybe if you take another look at what we want and if you can provide it, then come back to us." This was healing. Feeling a warm peace running through me as my power returned with the connection and acknowledgment of my experience, I thanked him for his time and left the room and immediately emailed another insurance company, who replied by return, no problem, leave it with us. By going through this situation I was no longer victimised by this particular childhood trauma that had been integrated into my being for years. This experience helped weaken the core belief I had running of not being good enough. For this I was so thankful.

You Gotta Feel it to heal it. Life continues to offer opportunities to heal the whole time. When we are triggered with an old emotional pain with openness and awareness, *we can heal and create a new outcome, if* we see these situations as the gifts that they are, it *allows a new healthier memory to be anchored into our cells and we stop running away from situations that we think may give us another similar experience.* Then we are freer and healthier to move forward without carrying our past pain and damage with us. Avoiding, denying, overriding, numbing out, or even trying to manage our emotional pain will result in us continuing to be triggered. Pain is buried deep in our cellular memory, which at the initial time of the trauma, we are often unable or not equipped to deal with it. We can get over this and even mentally understand what happened, but healing is different. Of course this isn't comfortable. Sometimes it's even painful, but by going through it at the other side we find peace, power and freedom. More importantly *we no longer are victimised by our past life experiences.*

*

When I was around fourteen, my father who had a bit of wanderlust, decided to move the family from our hometown and explore other parts of the world. Unfortunately, none of these attempts to re-locate were particularly successful, but on one occasion in the early seventies he did land a job in Malta. He and my mother went for a short visit and soon after their trip, sprung the news that our family would be moving there. The whole thing was badly planned and unstable from the outset. The moving date was changed a number of times and for a variety of reasons. One delay was because my father received a head injury after his drunken friends, in an attempt to mark his departure to a new life, threw him over a bridge into the local river, laughing loudly as they waited for the expected splash. Unfortunately the river water was low and instead of a splash they heard a crash as he landed on the rocks and stones below, their laughing turning to horrified gasps of concern. Luckily his injuries were not too serious and only required a few stitches in his head, but they were enough to delay our departure date for a few weeks.

A few days before we were due to leave, my parents informed my younger sister and I that we needed to ask our school teachers for homework, to keep us going for a period of at least three months. This request from my parents was beyond belief but they didn't see the point in enrolling me and my sisters in a Maltese school. The Friday before we were due to leave, on Monday morning, my younger sister and I, following our parents' instructions, we dutifully went to our teachers to ask for homework to bring with us to Malta. Nervous, knowing this was ridiculous we stuttered. "Errrr, we've to ask you to give us some homework that will last for a few months because we're going to Malta on Monday, can you tell us what to take." Each teacher had more or less the same astonished reaction. They looked at us as if we had suddenly grown another head, shaking theirs in bewilderment "Are you crazy? No, I can't do that. Aren't you enrolled in a school there? Tell your parents to send you to school."

We did not go to school in Malta. Instead, at aged thirteen and fourteen we were effectively taken out of all schooling to basically hang around. Obviously this happened at a pretty important time in our educational lives but although I was bored, I wasn't disappointed either, predominately because school was not my favourite pastime, not because I lacked academic ability, as I was in the second top stream, but because I was insecure and lacked any level of confidence. There was no way I was insisting on going to school.

My parents weren't home-school types of people. They preferred a 'pint' as my father would call his beer, or a 'nip', which was a shot of whisky. Mostly he enjoyed them as a couple, 'the nip and pint combo'. The trouble was, one usually led to another. It rarely if ever, was just 'a' pint, more often it involved us all being in the bar until closing, before driving us home, by then tired and irritable, to our rented apartment.

The resentment inside of me was building and was written all over my face. It oozed out of every part my being. I would sit in the bar surrounded by the adults who the more they smoked and drank would start a sing song thinking "I hate this." Now beyond anyone trying to engage me in a conversation I would glare sullenly thinking "Go away - just go away and leave me alone!"

Myself, and my two younger sisters, away from friends, with no real guidance or structure, were bored. As long as we didn't get into any trouble, things were fine but we did occasionally sail close to the wind and had some narrow escapes! One day my younger sister and I arrived home from a day in the park to find the door to our fifth floor apartment locked. With no idea when anyone was coming home, hungry and bored, we began to figure out a way to get into the house. It dawned on me that if we went onto the big flat roof of the apartment building where we dried our washing, we could go over the top and reach our veranda. The balcony door was never locked, so we could access the house through that door. Feeling excited and very smart at solving our problem, we climbed the stairs onto the roof to see the patio door open as usual. Encouraged with our success so far, the next step was to throw the washing line over the edge of the roof, slide down the rope, then simply jump onto our balcony. "Who's going down the rope?" my sister asked. "You" I replied. "I'm not doing that I'm scared, it's too high" she argued, "You go." I insisted that it was safer for her to as I was the strongest and she was the lightest so, she became the unwilling, fearful hero elected to perform this particular task. "It's okay I've got you, you'll be fine" I encouraged her as she climbed over the wall of the tall apartment block. Hanging on for grim death, she slowly slid down the washing line fearfully squawking and grumbling "Don't drop me, don't let go" until she thankfully landing safely on the balcony below. The memory of this still fills me with horror at the danger and devastating consequences that could easily have resulted, but at that time, we never gave it a second thought. Nowadays a child protection team would have a field day with us.

> Boredom is dangerous, it is like death to the soul and to feel alive again we can go to extreme measures and take risks that may place us in great jeopardy.

The whole situation in Malta was extremely difficult for me. I became depressed, angry, frustrated, and the grain of confidence I had, all but disappeared, leaving me wondering what life was all about. From my point of view, family life was pretty challenging. Everyone and everything was very intense and stressful, this period was the beginning of the end for me and bored, and depressed I began to over indulge on large slices of delicious bread made fresh daily at the local bakery, desperately trying to fill the emptiness inside. I asked to have horse-riding lessons, but they were too expensive. In need for stimulation and connection, I wrote endless letters to my friends back home, wishing I could be there too. My parents began to realise how difficult I was finding things, and not knowing what else to do, made the decision to send me back to Scotland. Luckily for me, a work colleague of my fathers was visiting Malta on business, and I was to travel home with him. I was thrilled but it was a stressful journey all round. The man was very polite, but a complete stranger and clearly didn't really wish to be burdened with babysitting an unhappy, sullen and depressed fourteen year old all the way to the UK. Once there I was to live with my elderly grandmother.

The night I arrived back from Malta I was exhausted and in bed just after 10pm, more than glad to be home in Scotland and happily looking forward to seeing my friends the following day. I was just about to drift off to sleep when I heard a strange noise coming from the street. It sounded like a whistling wind spinning though the air. It came closer and grew louder, then an icy chill filled the room. Not understanding what was happening fear gripped me, when I realized the whirling noise was right there in the room. Now petrified, I couldn't move or speak. One eye tightly shut, I squinted through the other and saw a cylindrical solid light on the wall above the dresser. The time was exactly 10.20pm. My mouth opened and closed several times in an effort to call for help but nothing came out, until a strangled screech eventually left my mouth "HELP something is in my room!" My granny came to the foot of the stairs and flicked on the landing light "What's happening?" I blurted out to my gentle old granny, that a ghost was in my room. Poor dear, her nerves were shattered talking about ghosts and such, just after I arrived. She reached for a brandy to calm her nerves, my aunt was called my uncle was called, the whole place alerted. They all decided that it was my imagination and it should be forgotten. I tried to do this, but that incident troubled me for a long time. For years after, every Friday evening at 10.20pm, anxiety would bubble up within me as I wondered if the "ghost" or energy would come back, but once the clock had ticked past the 10.30pm mark I was okay again. For the next fifteen years, I slept with a light on in my bedroom because of that one incident.

> Whatever our experience, whether understood by others or not, it is important to be validated, because for us it is very real. When we are invalidated, anxiety results and our self-confidence is impacted. We can begin to internalise, doubt ourselves and personalise situations, then we convince ourselves there is something wrong with us, exacerbating low self-esteem.

*

To all intents and purposes I had left home by the age of fourteen, living with my grandmother until she died. The day she passed away I was in her kitchen, washing my hair in the kitchen sink. My aunt and the doctor attending her were upstairs. My head was under the tap in the kitchen sink, rinsing my hair under the running water when I thought, "Oh, granny's just died." Five minutes later my aunt came down stairs with the news followed by the doctor. "Your granny has died" My aunt said "Can you take some coins change and go to the public phone box at the top of the road and call your mother and auntie and tell them what's happened?" She went on, "I'll go and put the kettle on." It was her usual habit in times of crisis to put the kettle on and have a cup of tea. While I was running to the phone box at the top of the road I wondered, "How do I say this" I decided I just had to say it, there was no easy way and I would deal with the response as best I could. I dialed the number and asked to speak to my uncle and my father.

After my granny died, it was decided that I move in with my aunt and cousins. The year I spent with my aunt was happy.

She was very maternal and kind. She loved taking care of people and I felt pretty safe there. But I was a lost soul and my overwhelming sensitivity and insecurity grew. With no ability to handle it, I began to shut myself down. The jarring pain of living in the world became too much, I needed help, and it came in the form of a bottle of pills. Valium became my friend, my answer, closing me down into a blissful emotional flat line, and there I remained for the next fifteen years.

Life became a crazy cycle of survival. It was no surprise and actually very normal for girls from my town, to marry young, and have children as soon as possible, regardless of how unhappy it made us. I was no exception; unhappy, insecure and beyond naïve, the belief at that time was that if you slept with someone, you had to marry them. It was only in romantic novels or movies that people had lovers or several boyfriends, or had any choice for that matter! Basically, we played at 'making house'. We were children having more children.

*

At sixteen I became engaged to a boy a little older than I was, but incredibly he seemed even more immature. We argued and fought a lot, and on more than one occasion the engagement ring was dramatically thrown back to him and the whole thing was called off.

His mother often stepped in, fought his battles and in general did everything for him. He was the youngest in a family of four and her baby, and had no real idea of what responsibility meant. Of course I was not much better, but I did grow up a little on the news of becoming a mother. We were not in love, but back then pregnancy meant marriage – it was a recipe for disaster from the beginning.

Like a lamb to the slaughter, standing with my father waiting to walk down the aisle in my pale blue wedding dress, handmade, by my mother and me, I quietly thought, "Go through with this. You have no other choice, but there's always divorce if it doesn't work out!" My thoughts on the day of my wedding were a shocking indication of where I was in terms of immaturity and a clear indication that I was marrying for all the wrong reasons.

> There are always other choices even though we may not be able to see them at the time. Usually we can't see them because they are too scary for us to consider.

The marriage was like a bad "B" movie and for the thirteen months I managed to stay, I was miserable. He continued behaving like a single man, going to the pub on a Saturday afternoon, gambling on the horses, playing darts on a Wednesday night - anything else was of no interest to him. My role was to look after my baby girl, paint and decorate and try to make a home.

It was an uphill battle and eventually the whole sorry situation ended dramatically one rainy night after yet another argument. These fights were not small heated discussions, they were physically, and mentally abusive, sometimes vicious, one terrible immature drama after another. That night however, it was one time too many, finally, enough was enough and I walked out, or rather ran out, into the dark rainy night, carrying my then ten month old baby girl to the phone box at the end of the road. There, hysterical I called my father to come and get us. It was over.

We were both happy to end the sorry, sad fiasco. Now at eighteen, a divorced single mother, I was under the illusion that I was all grown up. Experienced in the ways of the world, I thought I had been through the worst and what more was there to life? Hahaha, what a joke! My naïve belief felt 100% true and was arrogant beyond comprehension! However, everything is relative, and in relationship to the previous year, I guess I had grown a little? Parental Guidance, where were you?

This excruciating and ridiculously sad chapter of my life was too much to handle. Not knowing what else to do, as soon as the ink had dried on the divorce papers, I decided to completely erase the whole sorry situation from my mind, effectively removing it as if it hadn't happened. Denial became my answer to allow me to move on with my life.

> Avoidance and denial causes emotional and mental sickness and prevents any growth, change or improvement from happening. It keeps us emotionally immature. We deny the things that we are not ready to take responsibility for, usually because of insecurity, immaturity or fear, but denying our experience means we learn nothing from it - nothing at all. Stuck on the insane and sometimes painfully vicious merry-go-round called denial we continue to repeat the same behaviour until we get the lesson.

Unexpectedly fifteen years later the opportunity to be reminded of this part of my life came while I was working in a city store as a window dresser/display assistant. Busily concentrating on a store display, I felt someone tap my shoulder and ask me my name in the distinctive accent from my hometown. Surprised I turned around. She was completely unfamiliar to me, but I gave her my name anyway. A satisfied smile appeared on her face: she had it right. "I thought it was you! You used to live in the flat above me during your first marriage." She was a former neighbour. My hand automatically rushed to my chest as I gasped, trying to catch my breath, which was suddenly in short supply. My jaw dropped as a flood of memories deleted for years, washed through my mind. "Oh my, I had forgotten all about that!" She looked at me strangely - no wonder! Who the heck forgets that they were married? Apparently I did! My daughter from that marriage had been legally adopted by my second husband, and had no contact with her biological father. This was his choice, and it suited me. There seemed to be no need for the memory to live on in my mind it was best forgotten, so I had!

> Our minds have the power to block painful memories, but life always offers us opportunities to remember what we have denied. This allows us to learn and heal from those difficult experiences.

My girl decided she wanted to meet her father in her early twenties. Of course I got in touch with him and they met a few times. I did not interfere and left it entirely in her hands whether she would pursue a relationship with her biological father or not. She was in touch for a little while but no longer has any contact with him. Apparently she could not handle the immaturity.

Arrogantly believing I was all grown up, but in reality, I was still stuck in my old habits, desperately looking for the answer to happiness, and no more maturity or awareness than in my last relationship, at nineteen, I met my second husband and we married within three months. Yep, this is true, good grief what was I thinking? But at least this time I was in love.

A tall, handsome guy who played guitar in a rock and roll band, he even played at our wedding! For the next three months we enjoyed an extended and blissful honeymoon. We were happy and had a lot of fun at the beginning, he was a great father to my daughter and occasionally the wives would travel with the band to gigs around the country, which was a welcome change from the small town we lived in.

However, after about twelve weeks of wedded bliss, the storms of reality thundered in, hitting me in the face like pellets of ice rain with the realization that we had begun to have issues. He found responsibility difficult and a few months after we married he lost his engineering apprentice-ship, then he gave up playing in the band saying he was sick of the travelling, or maybe the band gave up on him. Now he had married, it seemed his ambition had all but disappeared - he felt he had everything he wanted. I felt pressure.

Within a year we had another beautiful baby girl but with no money coming in I took my first part-time job when the baby was three weeks old. Desperately trying to make ends meet and determined to make this marriage work, I did whatever needed to be done to keep our heads above water. I took on more part-time work, waiting tables, cleaning, sewing at home and babysitting other peoples' children; anything and everything I could to be a good wife and mother. The next ten years, were some of the most emotionally stressful, financially hard, times of my life, and a constant uphill battle. Sometimes I felt like it was held together with only chewing gum and pieces of string for support! Under all the pres-

sure explosive tantrums were frequent. Emotionally immature and not knowing how else to deal with these episodes,
tiptoeing around to 'keep the peace' became normal and also
extremely stressful.

> Tiptoeing on eggshells to avoid another person's reac-
> tivity sets us up for major stress. We try to keep the
> peace becoming passive/aggressive fixers, controllers
> and manipulative people pleasers and we are doomed
> to fail at our attempt to keep everything and everyone
> happy. Unable to keep any peace, especially within
> ourselves we are constantly in fear. We mentally jump
> ahead into future possibilities and try to plan for every
> eventuality or scenario to hopefully avoid the next
> problem. Worry and anxiety builds, as we go into over-
> drive, overthinking everything. With no time or abil-
> ity for connection to ourselves depression and/or anger
> builds and we try harder and harder in our efforts to
> 'keep the peace', sacrificing our hearts and souls on the
> never-ending wheel of failure. The damage we do to
> our already low self-esteem is immeasurable. Paradox-
> ically when things do breakdown, as they will, with no
> connection to the part we play, we secretly blame the
> other person, victimising and martyring ourselves in
> the process. Then guilt kicks in and the whole vicious
> cycle continues and we go back on our tiptoes.

When home from work he would lie on the floor, watching television, smoking his time away. Trying to bring in
much-needed routine, for the first five years I felt like a fifties
housewife, and truly did my best to accommodate everyone

and make our marriage work. By now we had another baby, a longed for son and also had moved to another part of Scotland, away from family. This was very difficult for him and he always yearned to go back home to his roots, often sad and frustrated if he didn't see his family enough. For me it was different. Being away from my old hometown was much easier, plus, our three children had many more opportunities where we lived now. Going back was not what I wanted at all.

During this time to avoid my unhappiness and lack of fulfillment, every minute of my day was filled up with doing, thinking or planning something or another. Walking on eggshells hoping to avoid any reactivity, the little confidence I had was shredded to destruction.

As a married woman with three children, I would go to the supermarket with my head down and not speak to anyone. Shy, himself - it made him nervous if I talked to people he didn't know. Consequently, it became very easy for me not to see anyone. Every tiny little event out of my comfort zone caused me massive volumes of stress.

Simple occasions like a neighbour having a Tupperware party would send me into a spin for days or even weeks. Feeling devoid of choice I would force myself to go, not because I wanted to, but because going was easier than saying no to the invite. The self-imposed agony suffered because of my inability to say "no" would consume me. My main concern was what other people would think. When I arrived, my priority was to find a seat in the corner and become as inconspicuous as possible. With my arms and legs crossed, my head down, not making any eye contact, my body language silently screamed "Keep away! Don't talk to me!" I'd sit there wishing it would end. "What will I say if someone talks to me?" An irrational dialogue spun incessantly in my mind telling me "No one is interested in what you have to say anyhow. You are not good, clever, or interesting enough for anyone to take any interest in you." More significantly I felt that the only thing I was interesting enough for was for people to talk about me and not in a nice way! Self-judgment ruled my entire life!

> **When we have low self-esteem and self-judgment this is automatically projected out towards everyone else.**

As the lady demonstrator did her thing, my ever-spinning mind jumped ahead into the future, formulating a plan on how to get out of there as quickly as possible. My judgment of everyone was astonishing, I was certain that everyone would be offended, and would talk about me when I left. Of course before leaving I would have to buy something just to fit in and to stop the imaginary gossips, so I would place a small order even although I could ill afford it.

Then came the hardest part. As she simply did her job the lady demonstrator would ask the guests to host a party as an incentive for the hostess to receive discounts. This whole situation caused me incredible levels of anxiety. I would rather eat my own arm raw than have a group of people in my house while I offered them sandwiches, tea and cakes. This was my own personal nightmare and the last thing I wanted to be involved with. My dilemma was excruciating. If I said yes, I scored major points with the hostess and everyone would like me and if I said no, my fears were confirmed and they would continue to hate me as I thought they did anyway. "Would you like to have a party?" Here it came, my worst nightmare descended into my reality. Did I say, No, sorry I can't have a Tupperware party for you in my house? Of course not! I was incapable of saying no to anyone, a chronic people pleaser my standard answer was always "Yes of course," to anyone, and anything! My people pleasing skills were honed to perfection and automatically I agreed to everything, constantly extending my agonising misery. "Yes of course, that will be fine," I agreed smiling, wishing the floor would swallow me up whole or in pieces, by now I didn't care how I left, I just wanted out. But unfortunately the floor wasn't obliging and wasn't eating me out of my misery so I continued to suffer in a different more excruciating way. It never occurred to me that I had any power at all so I enquired "When is the best time for you?"

> Saying no is one of the most empowering words we have. If we cannot say no to others, we will personalize when they say no to us. We unknowingly transfer our own self-judgment to others and waste an incredible amount of energy to come up with a story to get out of situations. Saying no is the biggest word we have to create healthy boundaries of respect around us. Our need for approval prevents us from saying no just in case we upset another by not doing what we think they want us to do.

Due to my complete lack of confidence and need for approval I was unable to be upfront and honest to the hostess and tell her I had no intention of actually having the Tupperware party. She might be upset, talk about me or not like me, dear oh dear! All manner of painful judgemental stories constantly ran through my anxious mind. There were other ways of getting out of this situation, most of them I had practised to a fine art. Excuses were abundant in the database of my mind, the most effective being sickness. As the date drew nearer I literally made myself ill. This gave me the perfect reason to cancel, and it came with the added bonus of a sympathy vote.

Being ill in those days wasn't difficult, I was actually sick a lot. Weekly visits to my doctor were usual, with aches, pains and symptoms of one ailment or the other. Prescribed medications were a big part of my diet and I had been on every type of pain killer and antibiotic available. Migraine headaches that lasted for four days were normal, fibromyalgia, flu, joint and muscle pain, kidney and urine infections, symptom after symptom, you name it I suffered from it. I could have been issued with a season ticket such was the regularity of my trips to the GP's office.

We use excuses when we are afraid to be upfront and honest. They are useful to 'dress up' the truth. Mostly though when excuses are used instead of mature honesty the people who hear our excuses actually know that we are not being honest. The energy of honesty is unmistakable - it is peaceful and clear; excuses are not peaceful, but unclear and leave a residue of doubt. We do not always recognise a lie but we will always recognise a truth.

Physical symptoms often occur when under major emotional stress. The physical body will pick up on what we are over riding. We are all experts in over riding our emotions, often afraid to feel them as they can be too over whelming. We have various strategies and once a label is recorded it is easy to take it on and become the label. It also gives us an excuse to not take responsibility for our lives.

At home our relationship had deteriorated. Often we didn't speak to each other for days and it had came to the point that when I entered the room he would leave and vice-versa. There was nothing left between us, we were ships that passed in the night. I now worked part-time in party plan, the very thing that filled me with horror only a few years ago but I found that I enjoyed meeting new people outside of my normal circle once I had overcome my fear. It was like I had stepped into a different role outside the home, and one that seemed to have a little bit of confidence. I found I could make people laugh which was a bit of a surprise as really underneath I was the extreme opposite. I was wearing a mask. But it did give me a little money of my own no matter, the inner debate of "can I really afford to buy this pair or tights or not, or what's the best route to take home that has the most down hills so I can freewheel the car and not use all the petrol" still played loud and strong in my mind. Living hand-to-mouth the children's needs were always my priority. Knitting, sewing, baking, my way through the days until it was time too load up my car with cane furniture and fancy goods and head out to meet people who I thought were 'normal' or happy. I knew there was more to life and wanted to have it. But I felt dead inside. My jokes were hiding the truth of how I felt. Something had to give and finally it was me, I got sick and ended up in hospital. A virus raged through me, my immune system shot. After ten days I was on the mend physically, but emotionally not so much! The spell in hospital had given me time to think. Now no longer in love I wondered, how can I go on, I was so done with the way my life was. The responsibility, the pressure, no fun, no money and no longer any love - I was only existing. Suffering - not living.

On my thirtieth birthday I arranged for the children to be with different friends and I recklessly went AWOL for a few days. Depressed and desperately sick emotionally, popping pills to make me sleep, out of control of myself I had a complete emotional collapse and made a feeble attempt to overdose but really it was just a sad despairing plea for something to change. At this point I didn't care about anything except being heard.

> **Whatever we are going through, whoever we are, we deserve to be acknowledged and heard. We all matter.**

This was a turning point. I knew that if I wanted to I could opt out of life and continue to stay sick, goodness knows there were enough problems on my medical records to guarantee that I need not work or be responsible for myself again. The other option was that I could get well. This was my conscious choice and another fork in the road towards self-discovery. Of course this was a wonderful decision, but little did I know that the road was to be long, rocky, winding and sometimes even treacherous, but worth every step.

> **One decision, however small can change the course of our lives and can lead to many more decisions that will create a new future and take us towards a new path.**

Both my husband and I agreed our marriage was over. He moved out and we both tried to move on. We battled for four years with the divorce until finally I surrendered and agreed that he need not pay child support for our three children. The divorce now settled, I was free, but now I was solely financially responsible for the children and myself. He was a good man but was simply unable to deal with life and handling pressure. Not the best situation when you have a wife and three small children, but now it was time to move on and make some changes.

> Making a decision to accept what we feel is not really fair must be done with the complete understanding that we are making our best choice based on the reality and all the facts, otherwise resentment can take over. Accepting does not mean liking, but if we make any decision to let go and move on we must focus on the benefit we are getting from the choice we have made. The other option of course is to carry on fighting, but we must assess if it is worth the energy we have to use in order to continue.

On the day my husband left, there was one lonely tea bag in the jar, no money in my purse, my oldest child was about to attend secondary school for the first time, my second continuing in primary and my third child about to start school. Clearly there was an urgent need for money to buy food, school uniforms, shoes, books, and simply to live. Quite bluntly we were on the bread line and I needed a job sooner rather than later! A friend of a friend told me there was a temporary position available in a whisky factory. My prayers were answered. I applied and was recruited. It was hard labour, but very importantly it brought much needed structure to my day, money into the house and food onto the table.

The job involved the many different processes of making whisky. Getting it from the vats, into bottles, then boxes and eventually distributed to customers. Once again I was surrounded by alcohol, immersed in it as we bottled, labeled, boxed, 'sighted' mopped and smelled of whisky. Sighting was particularly strenuous and involved lifting 40oz bottles of whisky by the neck, flicking them upside down into a box with a light at the back to view for flaws in the glass. A bell would ring to start and end the day. If anyone needed a bathroom break the supervisor would stand behind the person and say "Go now you have five minutes" Then it was a case of stepping away from the conveyor line at the same time she would step into your place. When I saw this happening I thought holy moley it's like being part of a machine, a well-oiled dancing machine where we are all non-thinking non-human cogs in the wheel. Every second counted we clocked in and clocked out on the bell and the time in between belonged to the company. It was hell, damaging my shoulders, wrists, hands and fingers, but well-paid hell! **Its amazing how survival can make us power through. The pain I experienced in this job also helped me to make another decision, pushing me to take an enormous step forward.**

Now a single parent with three young children, I was very aware that we couldn't keep living week in week out from hand to mouth, but my lack of education was a major drawback. I began to seriously consider going back to school as a mature student. This was a giant step and the idea of it quite frankly made me want to throw up, mainly due to my very strong belief that I was not remotely smart enough to even pass the entrance exam, far less any others. My opinion of my educational ability was now subterranean. It never occurred that it was possible for me to have a career, become a nurse, or a teacher, or whatever in fact, I was in awe of people with professional careers - to me they were incredible. Maybe if I was lucky I could possibly stretch to being a shop assistant, but any belief in myself was buried so far underground it seemed impossible to ever find it.

> What we believe we are capable of either limits or encourages us. We feel our beliefs are true and they feel real, but they are not actually true. Beliefs change as we open our minds to the limitless new possibilities available to us. If we can nourish the beliefs that all belief can change, it will help us to free ourselves from old limiting beliefs. Our conditioned beliefs run through our lives until we see the potential for something else - and there is always something else to see.

After a great deal of procrastination I finally applied to go back into full time education. Once this decision was made my next hurdle was to actually write the entrance exam. This was when my old delaying tactics came up like a comfortable old blanket, such as getting sick at the last minute, talking myself out of it and searching for any excuse possible to avoid the distress of stepping out of my comfort zone. But because the pain of my situation was greater than the pain of moving into unknown territory I consciously chose to ignore all of these old habits and put my big-girl pants on and just do it. Still, on the day of the test I had to drag myself kicking and screaming into the exam room. Sweat dripping from my hands as panic engulfed me, every ridiculous thought that came to mind was negative. "Who do you think you are, you'll never do this, you are stupid," but despite this, I eventually sat down and wrote the exam, fueled by the memory of the whisky factory with my damaged hands and aching shoulders underneath my pale blue uniform waiting for permission to go to the bathroom! "Hmm" I thought, "Just do what you can, you have nothing to lose and it could be your way out."

> Breaking things down into small steps makes it easier to overcome hurdles. Knowing your own strategies and tricks to avoid or delay and putting things in place to help you not use these tactics is helpful to the end result.

Being accepted onto my course was an incredibly pleasant surprise. Now officially a full-time mature student, and at last in a position to educate myself, I began to experience the world from a new perspective. It literally blew my mind to meet people from so many different cross-sections of society. It made me realise there was so much of life I had no idea about. My confidence was still very low, and speaking up in class, a major challenge but I was beginning to feel breath in my body, and also, for the first time ever, I was doing something real and positive for myself to improve my prospects, and I loved it. This in turn would help the future lives of my children. Until then, I hadn't realised how important it is for a mother, taking care of children, to also take great care her own emotional wellbeing and happiness.

> It is essential that we show our children how happiness looks and feels, by our own example. We have a tendency

to focus on giving them everything in an attempt to make them happy, meanwhile we are teaching them that we personally don't matter and our happiness is dependent only on theirs. This inadvertently puts pressure on them, especially if all they see is the stress, hard work, pressure and pain. As primary role models, a mother and father's influence on their children is enormous. Allowing children to experience their parents listening, resting, and taking care of themselves and looking after their own happiness as well as the happiness of their children, is much more effective than telling them how important it is.

The day I wrote my first English exam was a major milestone for me and something that I never thought would happen. Wild excitement overwhelmed me and panic took over. Waiting outside the exam hall my tutor came over and looked at me steadily in the eye "You will be fine – breathe" My flushed face with eyes popping out like deer in the headlights concerned her and she could see the potential that a full blown panic attack could erupt. "You must try to believe in yourself," she said. "Is she for real?" I thought "Me believe in me? Yeh right!" At the time I didn't believe it but in reality with every small achievement I had, my mind opened up more and I built a teensy little bit more confidence and self esteem, where before there was none, zippo, zero.

Each time we do something that we never thought was possible for us, we are stepping outside of our comfort zones and are building a stronger foundation in self-confidence.

I became interested in human behaviour and personal development while in college. Psychology was part of my course and this piqued my interest. At the same time my curiosity in spirituality developed, although mostly from a supernatural perspective. My fellow students and I spent many evenings talking into the night having long interesting conversations about the meaning of life, spirituality and energy. I always had a strong intuitive side, and ability to sense and read energy. Sometimes my friends would ask me to tune in and forecast or read situations for them and this seemed to be astonishingly accurate a great deal of the time. Despite my naivety and lack of solid grounding, somehow I was naturally able to get myself out of the way enough to allow guidance to land.

> Getting out of the way is being present. Being open, with no attachment to outcome. It means letting go of ego, with no need to get it right. It is an ability to listen from a neutral point with no judgment of what is heard and no need to fix or change anything. It is a connection to universal intelligence rather than our intellectual understanding. It is trust and knowing there is divine wisdom available to us, and if we get our egos out of the way, we can hear it and it will be guide us.

Personally, I didn't take any of this too seriously, but it did help me to feel more accepted than ever before. My biggest issue was always my insecurity. This form of my ego affected me in every aspect of my life and of course, impacted any level of clarity and insight. There certainly was a lot for me to unlearn and relearn but now I felt more ready and focused to do this.

Ego will show up in many forms, insecurity being a main one. Ego thrives on stories: the more dramatic the better, victimizing us as individuals or others. Victim is a powerful ego and is one of the biggest manipulators and controlling ego forms. Ego is not the bad guy until it takes over. We all need ego to get things done and to move us forward. It is important to use ego wisely and to not let it take over. It has protected us in our lives and so letting go of this protection is terrifying but until we do it, it will not be possible to connect to our authentic self and ego will be in charge of our lives, driving us with stories and fear. Love is often blocked when this happens.

Until I was in college my intuitive ability had never been explored or developed. In fact at the age of fifteen this big part of me was consciously shut down because I found it too much to handle. With no one around who understood or to give me any guidance, my only option to survive my own sensitivity was to stop feeling, period! I did this by using many different types of prescription medication to numb myself out. It also effectively ensured that I remained stuck in an emotional no mans land, going around in the cycle of habitual sickness. Now that this intuitive part of me was beginning to slowly open again, it felt strangely exciting. Knowing at last, that I needed serious help to heal, I reached out to whatever resources were available, including traditional psychology, friends and mentors. Opening myself to anything in order to get better, was a giant step, and although there was a long way to go, thank goodness the process had begun.

It is a big deal to ask for help and many of us don't, as we perceive it as weakness. Our fear of vulnerability is understandable as it has likely been exploited or taken advantage of at times in our lives. Therefore we must be wise with whom we ask to help us. When we are in the middle of our problems we can be clouded by our strong emotions and are not always able to see clearly from an objective standpoint, this is when it is useful to ask a neutral person who is trustworthy - that is, they are worthy of our trust because they have shown us over time that they deserve our trust. Never trust a person who is needy, insecure, loves drama or gossip, as they will be unable to be neutral, discreet or confidential as their drive for drama and need for attention or importance will make them unintentionally untrustworthy.

Things were improving but life was extremely busy and I was barely surviving by the skin of my teeth. I had no consideration or even the concept of how to love, value or respect myself and I lived a very disconnected existence. In addition to my busy life as a full time student and single mother, still under immense pressure to turn my life around, I often worked three part-time jobs to make ends meet; party-plan a couple of evenings a week, in a nightclub bar one night a week, then on Saturdays I had a sales job in a store. It wasn't easy it really wasn't easy at all.

Everything is relative and even a small baby step towards improving or changing something in our lives that is not working is still a step and will lead to another. The only step that is a problem is the one we don't take.

At the same time, I was happy to have started the process to give myself a chance and being in college, studying, and becoming self-sufficient, my confidence was building a little. My parents couldn't really understand why I was in education. In their opinion it was a waste of my time, and they constantly asked why didn't I just get a job? "Hello I have THREE jobs!" I wanted to scream angrily at the lack of understanding "Do you not get it?" No, they didn't get it! "What are you doing? You never liked school when you were growing up" they reasoned. Suddenly, a light bulb went on. It dawned on me that my parents could not give me any real emotional support. In fact truthfully, they had never really been able to offer this. It didn't mean they didn't care - not at all, they just didn't have it to give, so couldn't. It was a cathartic moment.

The support we need is always obtainable if we open up to all available possibilities that exist for help, but when we attach to it coming from a particular source, we can miss seeing the help or worse, we can reject it if it doesn't come from the source, people or place we are attached to it coming from. The consequence is that we feel the pain of disappointment, which comes from our attachments. Then we are locked into victimising ourselves as we perpetuate the story, that we are not good enough, loved enough or the classic, we are abandoned or rejected. In reality help and support will come to us, sometimes miraculously and from the least obvious and unexpected places, when we ask for it without attachment. It's natural to look for support from our parents, as it's the most obvious source, however,

> it is not always possible for them to give it. This doesn't
> mean they do not care as it is often interpreted like this,
> it simply means they do not have it to give or they are
> emotionally disconnected themselves.

As I integrated this information, peace washed through my mind, and I became emotionally more settled. Now I understood that it had been futile for me to attach my need for emotional support to my parents and then to my husband, when they just did not have it to give. This was a gargantuan epiphany and I grew up more in that moment than I had ever done before. It felt good!

> What we do not understand we judge. Judgment kills
> our ability to step out of our comfort zone. Fear of being
> judged does the same. As we awaken we must be able to
> fearlessly stand up in the face of judgment, our own and
> from others, in order to move forward onto our own
> path and create a life for ourselves that is honouring
> our own truth.

Life continued but it was a struggle with no support from their father, the financial responsibility for looking after them and myself was up to me. Bills piled in relentlessly. This helped me to grow in some ways but at the time it was a lot of pressure. The children would visit their father once every week, not always, but sometimes there was nothing for them to eat. Ever the fixer I would send some food supplies and a little cash with them to take the pressure away from them and him. They sometimes felt sorry for him and it was not unheard of for them to offer him their pocket money. Looking back on this time, I wonder how we all survived the crazy life we were living, but we did make it through, and my three children have turned out to be wonderful human beings, who I'm very proud of, even though their younger years could not have been the easiest. It was a hard, stressful, sleep deprived, crazy, character building, and tough life for all of us.

> Challenging times are our opportunity to grow and learn but this depends on how we see the situation. We can also become victimised by challenges if we give up or focus on blame. We play a part in everything that happens to us and if we can see this part and learn from it, we will grow.

During my final term in college I became very nervous about finding work, and to have something that paid money until I landed my 'proper' job, I decided to apply for anything and everything. A position as a display assistant/window dresser came up and I was offered the job on the understanding that the company agreed to give me time off to write my exams. My life was about surviving one high-pressured situation after the other and doing what needed to be done to keep our heads above water. Pumped with adrenalin, with no idea how else to do it, I kept all the balls in the air. There was no balance. In fact, there was no point of reference or experience of balance, but the main thing was, we were all okay.

> Balance creates wellness and life is constantly bringing us to imbalance. With any imbalance there is potential for sickness to develop. We can fall into imbalance very easily if we lose the habit of listening to what is true, right and what we need for our wellbeing in the moment.

After a couple of years on my own I met and became involved with another man. He was intelligent, handsome, and witty in a uniquely sarcastic way. Our first date was with a crowd of people and it surprised me to see the vast volumes of beer being consumed by everyone, subsequently being projected out in frothy mess, followed by a desire for more. It mesmerized me. Heavy drinking was a way of life where I came from, but watching people throw up then come back for more was another ballpark. I hadn't seen such dedication to drinking before and in my opinion decided this was drinking on a professional level!

Being around the consumption of large quantities of beer and wine raised the bar on my tolerance of alcohol once again, as I unconsciously normalised myself to the daily habit. What was I thinking? Clearly I wasn't, but I had simply reverted back into an extremely familiar vibration.

> The energy vibration that we are familiar with may not be healthy, but if it is our 'normal' it will feel comfortable. Because we understand it well, it resonates with us like an old familiar song that we can't get out of our heads, that even if annoying, we sing over and over again simply because we know it so well. This type of lifestyle had most definitely directly contributed to my low self-worth, insecurity, immaturity and lack of self-esteem, and it certainly confused and depressed me. At the same time, it was all I knew.

As most relationships where heavy drinking is involved, arguments, power struggles, control issues and of course the inevitable dramas come as part of the package. You name it, it happened. We lived a textbook, chaotic, co-dependent mentally, emotionally, financially unpredictable, crazy life.

It was during this time that my youngest child, my son went to live with his father. This was a huge decision for me and I struggled with it for a long time. Racked with guilt I felt a failure, unable to give him what he needed he was better off with his father who had at last moved back to his hometown. My oldest daughter was now in university studying to be a teacher and my middle daughter was still in school and lived with me.

It all finally came to a shuddering halt one memorable Saturday that started off in a fairly unremarkable way but ended being a life changer. In the early morning I left to drive south for a dental appointment and to visit family. Later in the afternoon just prior to driving home I called to let him know what time I would get back. I was unable to reach him but I talked with one of his work pals who assured me that my message would be passed on. Without a second thought and in blissful oblivion I set off on the ninety-minute drive home, unaware of the devastation that was to meet me when I reached my house.

My first indication that something was wrong was when I noticed my sister's car parked outside. It was strange as she wasn't in the habit of just showing up unannounced. My concern grew as a couple of worried looking neighbours waved over to me as I came to a halt and others were peaking out their windows as if they did not know what to say but wanted to see the drama unfold. Hmmm now I thought this is very peculiar. Beginning to think maybe someone had died, or something else equally shocking, I hurried to the door of my house. As I opened my front door a shocking chill ran over my whole body. My house was empty. Suddenly light headed, my stomach rose into my mouth then somersaulted back down, bursting on impact I felt its contents rise to my mouth again and again. Speechless, I gasped at the devastation before my eyes. Ashen as the blood drained from my face. I felt my eyes burn as they filled with fiery tears. In my now stark living room stood a forlorn and lonely plant, which seemed only to emphasise the vacant empty space, everything else that was home was gone. The fridge including contents was taken, the washing machine along with its plumbing gone, the telephone missing, everything vanished apart from my daughter's bed, and my bed.

This was not a sudden impulsive action; it had been planned to precision. Tuesday of that same week had been Valentines Day - he had sent me red roses. Two days later was his birthday and he happily received his birthday gifts from my family. The following day I attended a clinic appointment to discuss our second round of IVF so that we could get pregnant. I had been sterilized after my third pregnancy due to the risks as a diabetic, but after many tests the doctors agreed I was fit enough and we had already been through one round of this tough treatment. Now this?

That Saturday morning my daughter had left for her part-time job about an hour after I had. Once the coast was clear a squad of his mates had come into my home and moved everything out. The neighbours had not realised anything was wrong, but simply thought we were moving and I had gone on to our new house. When my teenage daughter had arrived home from her work and found the house empty, she thought we had been robbed and went to call the police but there was no phone. It was then that she ran to a neighbour to call the police, and the neighbor told her that he had moved everything. Of course, technically we hadn't been robbed, but we had been deceived and violated. My sister had been on a drive in the North of Scotland and had decided to come in. Thankfully she was there to help. The friend, who had taken my call earlier, was actually helping with the move. Not only had this guy humoured me on the phone, lying about what was happening but I later heard that he had found it amusing and gained some sick pleasure at my oblivion to what I would find when I got home. Betrayed, broken and defeated this was my rock bottom, and another loud and alarming wake up call. Up until this point I had not really paid any attention to the part that I was playing in any of my relationships, but merely survived and played out what was my 'normal'. I had lived in pain, drama and unconsciousness - now it was time to well and truly wake up.

This shocking and brutal wake-up call was my opportunity to make some big changes and now ready and willing to do so, for the first time I realised it was me who needed to do the changing! For years I had been falling for men who I thought the sun shone out of, and were the answer to my dreams and happiness then, I would try to change or fix them and, oh yes, change them to suit my needs! All of my attention was focused completely on them while I totally ignored myself, and then of course I lost myself. For the second time in my life my focus had to be on my own recovery, and this time on a much deeper level than before.

Having never even considered that I was part of the problem it was time to see that my insecurity, inferiority complex, anger, sadness, depression, fear, reactivity, personalization, people pleasing, neediness, arrogance, need to control, lack of value, love or compassion for myself, had anything to do with the way my life, my relationships, and my health and wellbeing were turning out.

That moment saw the beginning of one of the greatest and most difficult journeys any of us can ever embark on, awakening and sorting myself out was now my new priority.

It was the day I entered kindergarten in the life-long, never ending classes in the University of Life, where the teachings are to unlearn old habits and ways of living, in order to create a new future life and to change my personal history.

As there was nothing left, my first priority was to rebuild my home. With a lot of creativity and very little money, in a very short space of time, it was restored and more peaceful than before. This felt wonderful, safe and importantly, it was all my own.

It is surprising how quickly material possessions can be replaced. Losing most of the material possessions from my home taught me a valuable lesson in priorities. 'Stuff' used to be very important to me but this experience showed me that we can easily lose possessions, but they can be replaced just as easily, unlike people, love or time, all of which are irreplaceable and priceless. Never again would I worry about losing stuff. Even although I enjoy nice surroundings, if I have to choose between material possessions over emotional happiness, there is no competition. It was also a powerful teaching on how 'stuff' is not the answer to happiness.

Healing the emotional destruction and pain that had built up throughout my life was not as easy as putting my home back together. My already very low self-esteem could go no lower after the major devastating blow it had just received. As I trusted no one, especially myself, a very close friend suggested that I attend a 12-step programme for families of Alcoholics. Considering my history of being around heavy alcohol use, for large periods of time in my life, it seemed like a good idea. It helped enormously, and every day I religiously attended different groups, listening until I slowly began to understand a little better and things started to make more sense. My biggest insight was the role I had played in the dramas that had occurred and how I had added to them. Foolishly, up until then I thought the problem was always someone else's fault, after all I was the one who was holding everything together, so how could I be causing the difficulties? This realisation that I bore some responsibility was new and was initially met with some resistance. However, it began to sink in that by taking ownership for my part, I was given some power over my life, whereas before I had none. This was new and exciting.

Until we look at the part we play in the situations we find ourselves in, we cannot heal and are imprisoned as victims. As we take on board the responsibility for our part, the inner victim can run rampant, consuming us and take over, making us weaker. Connecting to this truth helps us to turn our lives on a new direction and inner strength begins to build. It is important not to confuse being blamed for something and taking responsibility for something that is actually yours to take. We all play a part in our experiences but we are responsible only for the role we play. In co-dependent relationships these roles become confused and blame is often thrown around and gets caught by the one who wishes to pick it up or is in the habit of feeling the most guilt.

Now with my focus directed towards working on my own life, there was an overall improvement in my mental, physical and emotional wellbeing and although headed in the right direction, it was sometimes one step forward and two back. There were days when I didn't want to get out of bed and couldn't manage to even crawl out from underneath the duvet as grief and dark depression consumed me, eating into my heart and soul. Unhealthy questions and dark thoughts played incessantly over and over in my mind "Why didn't I see this coming, what's wrong with me, why, why, why, did this happen?" I kept a big note pad beside my bed and wrote everything down, not even in sentences sometimes it was just a load of swear words on the page but it was better out than in. So little by little, slowly in tiny baby steps, with support from some very wonderful friends I dragged myself out of the black hole and began taking more control of my life. As the days and weeks passed I became stronger and fitter, I joined a gym and focused on my health and was soon, at least physically, super fit.

> When we are emotionally broken, a step towards healing is to move our body and exercise. This releases endorphins, makes us feel stronger and points us in the direction of our recovery. Then emotional healing can begin.

Soon the hurt and shock turned to anger. I no longer cared where he was, but if mail came to my house for him I used the opportunity to vent my rage and would scribble across the envelope a variety of venomous statements in red ink - "No longer at this address, try hell! Hopefully Hell," "Thankfully no longer here" or, "I don't know and I don't care." This gave me only a slight feeling of satisfaction before I dropped the mail back into the postbox. Much more gratifying was noticing that the more I looked after myself, the stronger I became, and surprisingly at the same time, my anger lessened. Making my own decisions I began to build a little more trust in myself, and felt a tiny fragment of more inner power.

> Anger is a powerful emotion, which is often judged as being wrong or bad, when in fact sometimes we have the right to be angry. It is what we do with our anger that is important. Anger is destructive when projected out at another or suppressed within us, but is a powerful and creative energy when focused towards making changes, to improve our situation in the world.

As far as I was concerned, I was moving on and that particular sorry chapter was over I believed I was done. It surprised me when one morning without warning, I woke up with the name of a street in my head and instinctively knew that the street was linked to him, and was possibly even his new address. Of course I had to check it out. Finding it on a map was easy, but hmmm okay what now? This information had been given to me, unbidden, telepathically transferred so should I listen? With very mixed feelings the next morning, I decided I had to investigate it a little further. Part of me was hoping I was wrong and it was just a meaningless thought. Another part of me did not want to know anything, but what made me more excited was that this hopefully was a sign that my intuition had come back. On my way to work, I made a detour and slowly turned my car into the telepathically delivered street name. Low and behold, there was his car parked outside a detached cottage at the end of the road! Now I saw with my own eyes the house that he had secretly bought for himself. Yay! Happy for a moment that this was confirmation my intuition was back on track. Content, I drove to work.

> The more we take care and look after ourselves, the stronger our intuition becomes. To look after ourselves properly we must listen to what we need – if we don't do this any intuitive abilities we have can be impacted and even distorted as our attention wanders to others. Even when we are working with other people we must connect with ourselves first before tuning in to anyone else otherwise the information gets mixed up and is then open to misinterpretation.

It had worried me for some time that I had been unable to see the shocking departure coming – I had been completely blindsided, but now it seemed the situation, terrible and cruel as it was at the time, was actually a blessing in disguise as these things can sometimes be. More than anything I needed to wake up, change my life, and stop living in denial and darkness. This shocking experience was my opportunity.

> Often our harshest experiences offer us our greatest gifts. When we are humbled or broken it offers us an opportunity to re-prioritise, re-assess and wake up to reality and awareness, instead of living in denial, avoidance and illusion.

Having lived with various levels of addictions for my entire life, healing and recovery was now my priority. I questioned myself "Was I up for the challenge to make the changes I wanted and needed for my life? Yes, of course! Hadn't there been enough suffering?" Even though I felt extremely lucky not to have become addicted to alcohol, definitely living with the affects of it meant I had a long way to go in my own recovery.

> The "ism" of alcoholism is a BIG problem and occurs when we have been in any type of relationship with a person who is addicted to using alcohol. The mental and emotional sickness progresses whether you are the person drinking or not. This means the mindset and behaviours that can develop while living with the influence of alcohol consistently around us need to alter in order to improve our life. Often these behaviours are passed down to us through the generations. They are sometimes very difficult to identify, because they are our 'norm', which means our family, friends and

culture have them too. When we are in the thick of this, trying to navigate the mental and emotional chaos that surrounds us, it's even more challenging to recognize. We develop survival mentality to protect ourselves, always anxious, stressed and on the alert, because we have to. Living like this is massively stressful and perpetuates the cycle. Usually when life is particularly difficult or painful, alcohol can numb the pain for short brief moments as we 'drown our sorrows' or 'relax'. The problem is, nothing is usually resolved, our sorrows haven't drowned, but are still there waiting for us once the affects of drinking wear off. Hurt comes screaming back, now bigger, stronger and with more intensity than before, plopping us into the endless rabbit hole of black depression and anxiety.

Unlearning the habits of a lifetime is a huge commitment and requires dedication and vigilance. My life quite literally depended on my ability to heal. Would I be able to go the distance? I hoped so. A day at a time they say, but soon I came to understand it is often a millisecond at a time!

In addition to attending the Al-anon 12-step program I began exploring what I called my 'weirdness'. A friend of mine finally persuaded me to attend the local Spiritualist Church and for the first time my psychic abilities were welcomed and I met people who understood. It was a major relief for me to know that I wasn't entirely alone or crazy and they too could communicate with 'unseen' forces and energies.

> To survive my teens and twenties, I had closed down my sensitivity and my intuitive ability by using prescription medications. Now, it was time to allow that door to slowly open again.

Soon I became very involved in the development circles where any psychic, clairvoyant or clairaudient ability was developed, encouraged and supported. There was a lot to learn. My biggest lesson was how to create boundaries because I had none whatsoever, and like a sponge soaked up energy from many different sources and realms, until it all got too much. I was not equipped or experienced enough to deal with the energies that clung to me.

One situation got a little out of hand when I felt a young boy around me, quite literally haunting me. I felt pressure around my head the whole time. One of the mediums from the church tuned in and said it was someone I knew, a young man who had recently passed away. That night when I got home I rang my father. "Can you check to the local papers for news if anyone young had died from a head injury recently." He answered immediately "Oh yes it was in the paper last week". A guy I knew when I was young had fallen outside a nightclub and hit his head on the pavement and he died a few days later. Oh my! I was bombarded and still had to learn the essential lesson of boundaries, but at that time I had no understanding of the importance of boundaries on a physical level, therefore how was I to understand the importance of boundaries being applied to the metaphysical realm?

> Personal boundaries are essential to bring us respect, with each individual responsible for placing their own.

> We need to enforce them on an individual moment-to-moment basis. Our boundaries will tend to change with our personal circumstances, and with the many different people who show up in our lives. Physical or non-physical, seen or unseen, the same rules apply - boundaries keep us safe, respected and healthy. This is important information as eighty percent of what is around us is unseen but very real, and not everything on the unseen metaphysical level is peaceful, kind and loving.

My awakening was the beginning of a long mountainous path. There seemed to be a bottomless pit of habits and behaviors still to unlearn, but there was no turning back now. It was not easy. At the beginning constant vigilance can be hard work. Sometimes I would yearn to go back to sleep and return to unconscious life again. However going back was no longer an option. It would only return me to 24/7darkness and the pain of living in hell.

Now I was on a different road, slowly, inching forward in another direction instead of whirling around in circles as I had done for years. Don't get me wrong I was still in darkness but everything is relative and in relation to the previous year I was more conscious, but relative to the limitless potential available, I was like a 4-watt bulb, but there were moments of occasional light now. The tests on the awakened road are constant and in the following months I was to find out just how much work there was still to do!

> Being awake comes with a lot of responsibility but the majority of people can only handle a little at a time as

we slowly and wisely build strength. Often people begin their journey of awakening but resist each opportunity for deeper consciousness as ego protects itself with massive resistance to change. Frustration and defenses often show up until once again pain forces the issue. We are tested over and over again to strengthen love for our souls. Our job is to never give up and see each test as another opportunity for more growth.

A few months later, when I was mentally clear, physically strong, and emotionally stable, for closure, and my own peace of mind I was ready to face him. Feeling a new level of confidence, I parked my mini outside the hotel where he worked and walked into the reception area. The news of my arrival spread throughout the building like an out-of-control bush fire. Most of the staff knew the situation - it had kept the gossipmongers busy for some months, a few had even been involved with the 'move.' Now there was more juice added to the drama to chat about over their spritzers. Would I cause a scene? Was I going to flip out? Their concerns heightened as much as their tongues wagged. But my intentions were clear. I wanted closure: nothing more and nothing less.

I was there for myself, and my own peace of mind.

Unperturbed by the jungle drums spreading the word that something was going down, I confidently walked through the door and no one tried to stop me.

After months of building myself up, I was fit, strong and clear headed. He, on the other hand, not so much! He looked strained and uncomfortable. However, how he was doing didn't concern me, because I had worked hard and was in a better place than ever before and felt free from the past. I also believed this to be my final step. We sat in his office and I asked my questions. "How on earth could you do what you did?" I wasn't angry anymore and at the end of the day, this information actually didn't really matter now, anyone who was able to go to the lengths he had gone was either very desperate or very determined, or a combination of both and maybe more. But I did have to ask just to see what his response was. "I didn't know what else to do" he said honestly. "You didn't know what else to do, there were lots of other things you could have done!" I said suddenly frustrated. Then I realized my job was to let it go once and for all. More peaceful and stronger, my closure complete, I left. If he felt any relief with the communication between us, it was of no importance to me. Genuinely wishing him well, I turned and walked back out through the door. I felt stronger, freer and more acknowledged than I had in a long time. I had held my own and felt more whole and healed because of this.

> Forgiveness has nothing to do with anyone but us. It is for giving us peace. It is letting go of the painful story and no longer suffering. When we face our fear and our painful past, it no longer has power over us.

This was a massive step for me. During our relationship my attention was constantly focused on him, making the mistake many of us do. I was always down at the bottom of the priority list, or more often, not on the list at all! This led to me often screaming for attention as I was left feeling insignificant and taken for granted.

> This very common complaint of always being left to the last before our needs are considered causes untold

> heartache. Putting ourselves, at the top of the priority
> list, not all the time in a narcissistic way, but sometimes
> in a balanced value and respect way, is essential for
> love, honour and respect to grow in our lives. When we
> always leave our needs to the end we send a message to
> ourselves that we don't matter. This perpetuates our low
> self-esteem, and the message we send others is the same
> thing. To create a healthier relationship with ourselves
> we must be the priority at least sometimes.

As time passed I became more certain I was home and dry until the test eventually came about nine months later. I failed miserably. Oh yes! Unbelievable as it seems, like the addict going back to drinking after years of sobriety, I had a slip. Completely sucked in I was seduced by new possibilities. I chose to ignore everything I knew, and once more stepped into the illusion, the game of avoidance and denial. He came looking for me as he needed my signature for a joint thing that we had and we got talking. I was so much stronger in my life but was still living in hope that I could find love and was still searching for it outside of myself. I still had a long way to go, as I was to find out.

> Living in hope is not the same as living with value and
> certainty. Hope is a wonderful and necessary compo-
> nent on the road to recovery. We all need hope in our
> lives, but it is not enough to live in hope alone. Hope
> is only the beginning. From hope we need to build
> certainty. If we are lying on the ground feeling hope-
> lessness and we find hope, it can bring us the strength to
> stand up and raise our foot into the air to take the next

step. This is hope but for us to continue walking forward we must build certainty, trust and inner strength. When we are living in hope we still believe that some-one else has the answer to what we need because they have given us something we didn't have at times when we most needed it, but it must eventually come from within ourselves.

All the reasons why we didn't work out before were ignored - co-dependency, need, immaturity, sickness and heavy alcohol consumption, the problems were made about everything else – it was the house, the neighborhood, the this the that – denial came in like a dense fog blocking any level of honesty, reality or clarity. Then to add to the situation I found a small cyst on my breast, which thankfully turned out to be benign, but nevertheless I had to have surgery four days before Christmas. I was vulnerable and he took care of me, cooked lovely meals for me and I before I knew it, I was hooked. Convinced this time that things would be different, I was lured by the promises of new beginnings. Before long we were living together again. Seriously, I had been in and out of this relationship like a fiddlers elbow, back and forth, back and forth, playing the crazy drama filled addictive dance, whizzing around on the all too familiar merry-go-round of "ism". Holy Moley! Clearly I still had lots to learn, but would I ever?? Profuse cursing springs to mind at this point, but I won't, just saying….

Relative to how it had been there was an enormous improvement in my self-esteem, but my relationship with myself was still not in a strong or healthy enough state not to lose myself again when tested. Unfortunately, because of this, I fell into the trap of arrogantly thinking that I was stronger than I actually was. The old familiar energy vibration of addiction was still powerfully playing out in me and was a lot stronger than the love, value and respect vibration that I had begun to build. Unknowingly, this placed me in danger and I became less vigilant with myself. Soon my focus went back to my relationship with him, instead of concentrating on building a stronger healthier relationship with myself. Our most important relationship is the one we have with ourselves. Unless we have a balanced loving kind relationship with ourselves it is difficult to have one with another person. In any relationship we are 50% of the whole. If our 50% is not clear, healthy, loving and kind, we will try to get that from the other person. Our responsibility is to take care of our part and let the other person take care of theirs. This allows the relationship to develop in a healthy, non-co-dependent way.

During this time, another of the many significant, life-changing experiences I was prone to having occurred while holidaying in Cyprus. We booked a mini cruise to visit Israel and Egypt and once it was confirmed that I was heading for Egypt, an indescribable excitement engulfed me. It felt as if my soul was returning home. As the ship sailed down the Suez Canal the desire to leap off the boat and kiss the ground was almost impossible to contain. The smile on my face stretched from ear to ear. My heart sang as I breathed in the atmosphere of the land, hungry for more. Enthralled by the whole experience, we visited the Great Pyramids at Giza and the Egyptian Museum in Cairo. The day in Egypt was the best day ever, and everything, and I mean everything, fascinated me.

After the amazing tour to Giza, back on board the ship and still feeling a warm glow in my heart, for no logical or rational reason whatsoever, an overwhelming urge came over me to talk to one of the tourists. Okay now what? It was a passenger from the ship who had stood out to me the day before. I had no idea where he came from, who he was, or even what language he spoke, but what I did know was I wanted to talk to him. As if some magnetic force was driving me to look for this stranger, feeling slightly insane I began to search the ship until at last I spotted him sitting on a lower deck enjoying the view of the ocean with a friend. Phew! I heaved a huge sigh of relief, but my stomach churned, spinning in cartwheels as I wondered what was next? I sat down on a chair close by, with my back towards them waiting. Of course next, I had to approach him. The energy increased, pushing me into action. This was not going away. With no inkling as to what to say, I rose to my feet and walked over to stand behind their deck chairs and gently tapped the stranger on his shoulder. He turned round to face me. My mouth opened and out the words tumbled. "Excuse me sir, I hope you don't mind me talking to you, but I need to ask you a question." "Yes" he said looking at me curiously. Now unable to stop the flow I continued. "You are probably going to think I'm crazy, but can I ask? Are you a spiritual healer?" Hearing myself say the words I thought "REALLY Oh my! What am I saying"? He looked at me steadily, and replied, "As a matter of fact yes, I am a spiritual healer, are you"? Breathing in another big sigh of relief I replied "Err no, no I'm not, I mean I can sense things and I know stuff sometimes..." I blabbered on trying to clarify, "But no, no I don't do any healing." He held my gaze for a few moments then spoke quietly with authority, "Well you really, seriously, need to do something about this." Smiling and nodding in agreement but with no idea what I "really seriously" needed to do, I thanked him for the short but meaningful discussion, and left.

At that time, my job was in sales. Being a 'healer' was not remotely interesting to me, and to be honest I was having a hard enough time trying to sort my own self out, without getting involved with trying to help anyone else, thank you very much! The strange conversation I had initiated seemed to be an acknowledgment or confirmation of something, although what, I couldn't begin to guess. The only thing clear was the short meaningful discussion satisfied me somehow and I had done all I needed to do for the moment. This was not a "nothing" experience, but was significant and special - why? I had no idea!

This unusual encounter stayed with me. It appeared that somehow a spiritual message had been delivered to me. On one level this made sense, but on another, was way out there. My life wasn't conducive to 'spiritual healing' at all. But it seemed somehow I had been given a key to a door deep within my soul. Possibly it would lead towards other options for my life, the bigger question was what these options were, and how would I do it?

Not fully understanding spiritual laws, I was still trying to work everything out intellectually. My mindsets were still coming from a place of ego, fear and judgment, needing to know when, what and how things were going to work out. My ability to truly listen and trust my guidance was not fully developed because I hadn't built a strong enough connection to myself. Everything was being filtered through the many old limiting beliefs systems rooted in fear still to be unlearned.

> Spirituality has different laws than our man made rules, beliefs and habits. Trust, faith and love and the ability to listen to a deeper truth is required to live spiritually. It is important to be open and willing to explore and question our beliefs without judgement and fearlessly face our fears in order to bring spirituality into our real everyday lives and not keep it separate.

In my search for answers to the meaning of my life, I was willing to try anything, and arranged to meet a guy who did energy readings. During my reading he told me I was a teachers' teacher and that I had much spiritual work to do. If he had been speaking Swahili, it would have made more sense to me! He gave me a tape with the recording of his reading labelled with the date and time. Unfortunately, the tape disappeared for three years.

> The rules and conditioning we learn in the physical world do not apply in the spiritual world. Intellectually understanding the vastness of universal intelligence is almost impossible for our small ego minds. Once we come to accept this, and learn to listen, we can move forward into a deeper spiritual life where trust and faith rule.

Life continued to twist and turn in unexpected and unusual directions, none more surprising than when my partner decided to buy a restaurant in my hometown and wanted us to move there together. This was the last thing in the world I was interested in doing and I did not see how this would be a benefit for me. The big guns were engaged "Why don't you invite your sister and her husband for the weekend?" he asked. Excited at this unusual offer "Okay" I said a little taken aback "That would be really nice." "I'll cook us all a nice meal and we can all catch up," he offered smiling. During the meal the topic of how nice it would be if I lived back in my home town came up "You should come back" both my sister and her husband persuaded "You work as a rep so you will be travelling anyway, then we can do this more often. It'll be fun." Against all that I held pure and sacred, the people pleaser in me showed up standing firm and prevented the "No" that was screaming loudly from my heart to be heard.

And so before my feet could touch the ground, I was persuaded to return to the place I had happily left over twenty years previously. On the first evening after the move, returning from my day job as I drove into the town, anxiety began to rise in my chest. Within seconds, I was parked at the side of the road, hyperventilating, triggered into a full-blown panic attack. What was I doing here, what had I done, why had a made the decision to come back? I loved my life in the north, I had lots of spiritual friends and connections, a decent well-paid job that I enjoyed, owned my own lovely little house, my life there was good, but most importantly, I had my independence. The only spirit that I was connected to here was the spirit of vodka or whisky. I did not need this, did I? Apparently yes,

I did. It was to take me another three agonising years to find out why.

Those three years were tough. My life revolved around working in the bar and restaurant at weekends. I changed my company job a couple of times during this period but eventually found a good Monday-to-Friday job in sales covering all of Scotland for a London-based company. This often meant that I drove between a thousand and fifteen hundred miles in a week, then at the weekend I regularly worked from 10am until 3am the following morning.

On Saturdays I was front of house for the lunch session after which, we got ready for the evening dinners. During the couple of hours I was home in the afternoon, the laundry was taken care of. This was usually a ton of dish and tablecloths to wash and iron before heading back for evening dinners. Sunday mornings were spent baking cakes and scones for high teas before serving the aforementioned high teas in the afternoon. Superwoman didn't get a look in. The only things missing were a pair of red knickers over blue tights and a cape.

Unknowingly, I had made myself indispensible and had created a need to be needed. It was co-dependence personified. Also I did not realize I was on one giant ego trip!

When our level of self-esteem and value is low, needing to be needed gives us a sense of importance, as we gain lots of attention and approval from others. This feeds our ego, but it is short lived and our ego needs more and more. This leads us to work harder and harder, to satisfy our need for approval and attention. This becomes necessary and our way of feeling good about ourselves because we pay little, if any attention to our own needs.

Basically we ignore ourselves and place the needs of everyone else above our own. Consistently settling at the bottom of the priority list, we become martyrs and victims without realising it. Unfortunately this often results in being taken for granted, which reduces our self worth even more, and causes co-dependency, and disempowers everyone. As our lives become more and more imbalanced we can easily get physically sick - mentally and emotionally we already are. The cycle is perpetuated, as our desperate need for recognition and approval from others increases. We become fixers, controllers and manipulators in a never-ending cycle we are helpers who are unable to see that we are not responsible for the lives of everyone, and at the same time, we are completely distracted from our own lives that are becoming more and more out of control and unmanageable.

Eventually, sickness crept up on me. My body ached constantly with pains in my hands, feet and shoulders. Sleep was impossible, without painkillers and being propped up in a sitting position. Headaches, backache and 'pain in the neck ache' were constant. My life was spinning in circles out of control, once again on a crazy merry-go-round. I was only just surviving, but did not know how to stop or alter it. Quite literally I felt I was a slave to the business and being taken for granted in a big way. Something had to change, and soon.

It is easy for us to override, numb out, ignore or disconnect from our emotions. Our emotions are connected to our physical body and if we continue to ignore ourselves emotionally, our physical body will force us to feel the pain we are over-riding or denying. A lot of the time physical pain is actually rooted in our emotions. Because we are less comfortable with ourselves emotionally, we then focus on the problem being physical and treat it as such, when actually the real problem could be our emotional pain and disconnection.

A short time later I had a small taste of reality and I woke up a little more to what I was dealing with. Early one morning after walking my dogs, preoccupied with what needed done that day, I slowly came down my garden path that faced directly into my kitchen when my eyes were drawn to the top of my kitchen wall cupboards. There lay piles of empty beer cans hidden from sight from inside, but as plain as day from the garden path.

This jolt of reality made me realise that I had to focus back to my own healing journey. After months of disconnection, denial, darkness and attention to everything and everyone but myself, the process of bringing spirituality, and healing back to my own life began again. I returned to the Al-Anon 12-step program, started meditating, listening to my spiritual music and registered for many different types of healing workshops and seminars. Searching for any type of help available, I engaged the assistance of many different types of people, African Shamans, a lady who was a keeper of crystal skulls, Celtic Shamans, Native American Shamans, Celtic

Seers, Esoteric Mystery School, Angel workshops, searching for answers, you name it, I tried it.

It was a beginning, but I was still looking outside of myself for answers, and not seeing what was right there in front of me. I had become a 'seeker' and not a 'seer.' The difference is night and day, but it was another step towards finding myself once again.

> Searching for answers is an essential step in our spiritual journey. It shows us that we are opening to question our old beliefs, but because we are searching outside of ourselves and not looking within, we keep searching. When we go within ourselves, we become aware. Ego is always searching outside for more attention, likes to keep everything separated, needs to play games, tell stories, be in the future or the past, and likes to compare, makes things right or wrong, needs to prove itself and has to be right every time!
>
> Ego is dissolved in the present moment and in humble vulnerability, which is another word for simple honesty. Ego often sees and judges humility as weakness. Ego speaks, the soul listens. The soul has no need to search, because the soul knows the answers it requires in the moment. The soul sees without judgement, need or comparison, and neutrally accepts the reality, with compassion and love.

Listening to myself became my daily practice, and then one day while working in the far north of Scotland, I rustled through the glove compartment of my car for some music to play, and there it was - the lost tape. **Incredibly, found exactly three years later to the precise minute, day and time it had** been recorded. Wow I was blown away. I sat in the car staring at the date written on the tape not knowing what to think. It was as if my life had been on hold, off the road and parked up in a layby, not moving forward for some reason for exactly three years. As I listened to the recording and the voice saying I had another path to walk, it gave me hope. Maybe the time was drawing near to go in another direction. The trouble was, I felt well and truly stuck in my situation with no idea how to get out of it, and to be honest I was scared to rock the boat or make a move. The fear of leaving and having a really tough time held me prisoner.

> We will not make the changes we want to if the pain of staying is less than the pain of leaving. When the pain of leaving is less than the pain of staying we will take the steps necessary to make the changes we want for ourselves. Pain is guidance and often our motivator. We do not like pain as humans but we need it to see what we are in denial of, or are avoiding taking responsibility for in our lives.

Although once again on my inner journey of recovery and self-discovery it was still secondary to the demands of the business, my job, and my partner. Still in the habit of over-giving, my recovery would often go on hold as other priorities came in that seemed to be more important than my wellbeing, happiness and health. Although there was some improvement, I was still a big people-pleaser with a major tendency to override and even ignore the things that were important for me.

Until I made my own healing a priority, it would not be possible to truly move forward and I would continue going around in circles. My spiritual practices were helpful, but they were more of a distraction away from my painful reality than making real inner changes. Until I connected to myself on a deeper level I was merely putting a plaster over the symptoms, rather than healing core issues

Chapter 3.
On the Road

It's fair to say up until this point that I had made some bad life choices, or maybe a better way to say it was that I was unawake to any real awareness or consciousness. I had been strong and survived a number of very difficult situations that had brought me to this place, but there certainly wasn't any real value or respect operating in my decisions. Life was still a question of survival, but now here I was, in a hotel relating my sorry tale to a man I barely knew, unaware then, that this person would help me find my inner strength and confidence, accept me, show me how to have value for myself, that would forever change my life. His support would encourage me to really and truly embrace spiritual healing and begin to live a life embracing and honoring my own spiritual truth but at the same time, I would have to be open and willing to do this.

It was becoming more obvious that each significant relationship I had been in was a reflection of where I was with myself internally, and all of them were an opportunity to grow and learn from. It is often the case that our partners are a reflection of who we are. They show us aspects that we may need to see or access within ourselves. These may be qualities that we admire or qualities that we don't like, but need to see and connect with to ourselves.

To my surprise he didn't judge. "Well there you have it!" I said nervously wondering what he was thinking. He had a poker face throughout the whole thing. I wasn't paying attention to him though; I was concentrating on speaking, just getting it all out. "What do I think?" he said then shocked me by saying "If I could bring everything you are together and describe you in one word it would be sunshine." Speechless with my mouth opening and closing trying to find a word, any word but nothing came" Come on I thought "Sunshine. Are you kidding me?" This blew me away! Then he tried to kiss me but I wouldn't go there. Nothing of that nature was going to happen. I was still wearing my invisible chastity belt and I was not going in that direction for now, if ever. Instead exhausted, I lay on top of the bed fully clothed and fell into a fitful sleep. I heard the door closing quietly as he left and went to his own room.

The next day I met with a colleague of mine for a meeting and coffee. We had parked our cars outside a hotel and were inside chatting, not knowing that our company cars were being broken into and robbed. My overnight bag was stolen and my colleague had her company phone and other valuables taken. We were in trouble and began to look around the car park frantically searching for our things. Unbelievably, my overnight bag was lying on the grass with all my possessions inside, however my colleague's things were gone, it didn't make sense. Someone was looking after me.

> We can share identical situations with others, but the experience is often completely different for each person. None of these are wrong and is a unique teaching opportunity for each individual.

Later I called to tell him about the break in. "Are you okay?" he asked, concerned. "Yes I'm fine." "I hope this is not a sign there's a bad energy about our meeting." He asked this not as a question, but more as an opening to the possibility. I assured him that all my possessions had been returned, as if it hadn't even happened, and then we went on to talk about the previous night and how much we had enjoyed each other's company. "Yes but I missed out!" I exclaimed without thinking. "What did you say"? He asked, wanting more clarity. Repeating myself I said that I was aware I had missed out on a night of probable mind- blowing unbridled passion. There was silence for a moment as my words sank in. Maybe he was also a little shocked by my openness considering I wouldn't let him even kiss me. Then he spoke "You are not ready, but that's okay." Now was my turn to be silenced with his next comment - "It's really weird but I just wanted to lie beside you and be in your energy." Huh? My mouth gaped open once again speechless I thought "Who the heck is this guy?"

Christmas came. He went to his hometown to visit his family. Bearing in mind we had known each other for a few weeks and had only been together for short times on the rally and one night in the hotel, it took me aback to find as soon as he left for his holiday, my heart felt it was really missing him. It was the strangest thing. When I mentioned this to him when he got back from his Christmas break - he said he understood.

The heart has the ability to transmit and pick up energy vibrations. The heart listens and feels connections to other hearts, which often make no rational sense to our intellectual minds.

A few weeks later I found myself in the restaurant bar, having to work for a staff member who had not shown up. It was 1am in the morning, and I had been working the whole day and was now surrounded by a heaving mob of party people who were dancing, drinking, shouting rather than talking, generally making merry, having drunken fun in the loud disco. Watching the scene from behind the bar, while serving alcohol and beer as fast as possible, it dawned on me that I was not being impacted by any of it. A strange peace surrounded me within the chaotic party setting, and for the first time I had no emotional charge or panic, and instead I felt neutral and unaffected. In that moment a quiet thought slipped into my heart "I can leave now." In the loud and teeming bar full of party people clambering for more alcohol, I had peace.

Once the lessons are learned we feel resolved and peaceful. Then it's good to go. We can leave.

A few months later during a break before the evening shift, I had a sudden urge to clean out my wardrobe. Piles of unwanted clothing were thrown into a bag ready to drop at the charity shop while the clothes I was keeping lay neatly folded on my bed, ready and organised to go back into my cupboard. It had been a normal day with the usual pressure, stress and strain, or some other minor occurrence that had escalated into yet another drama. The familiar tension hung in the air like poisonous gas but was nothing unusual.

Clearing out my wardrobe had felt therapeutic and was doing something for me. As I looked at the piles of neatly folded clothes lying on my bed, out of the blue I wondered, "Hmmmm shall I put these back into the wardrobe or will I pack them into a suitcase?" The question was answered naturally and easily. My bag was packed half an hour later and I walked out of the door for the last time. It was as simple and easy as that.

I was done. No more persistently banging my head against a brick wall, fearfully hanging on to a life that was no longer working for me. It had to change. I was tired, exhausted and I'd had enough. Suddenly I had the strength to leave, and for good this time. My life here was well and truly over. That night I found a bed in the spare room of an old school friend. It was time for a new beginning.

Within a short time, I had my own space with a new commitment to becoming a happier person. Creating a new life was my entire focus. A lot of old pain had accumulated over the years, locked into my cellular memory. Now a sense of urgency pushed me through many difficult, sometimes painful cleansing and healing processes. One after the other, I released this dead, stagnant energy on the cellular level. For the next three years I travelled anywhere and everywhere to work with anyone who could facilitate deep cellular healing.

Cellular healing is deeply intensive energy medicine and healing process. It supports healing at the core level, the cells. Held in a sacred space created by the facilitator, trauma, old mindsets or conditioning that has been passed down generationally, culturally or personally taken on. It is then connected to and intensified then supported to unwind and release on a cellular level, bringing balance, clarity and peace as the energy is able to flow freely without being blocked or restricted. This process allows mental, physical, emotional and spiritual expansion.

This intense inner cleansing process often kept me in bed for days, as I slept around the clock while the cells of my body recovered from the powerful emotional, energy healing I was working through. Layer after layer of trauma cleared, followed by another then another.

Dabbling with my healing was no longer an option, and no more a hobby or distraction but a serious commitment to healing every aspect of my being. It was the real deal and not fun, comfortable or relaxing. Often I experienced excruciating pain as the trapped negative and sick energy from personal, ancestral, and cultural experiences began releasing from the cells of my body and came to the surface to be freed. Moving into this type of healing is not for the faint-hearted, but this level of work can change lives. It offers freedom and empowerment but it involves enormous sacrifice of ego, unlearning old conditioned beliefs, and takes immense courage and humility to go through the deep transformational healing processes.

During this time, I was supported by a wonderful older lady, who became a dear friend, and mentor. She guided me with great love for many years. Don't get me wrong she was a kick ass and called any BS in a heartbeat. Tough love is still love!

Tough love is often the most difficult type of love for people to understand or recognize and is often judged. To the unaware it can look like the person giving tough love does not care or may even be being abusive. Sometimes stepping back and doing nothing is the kindest most loving thing to do. Enabling is well-intentioned help, and on one level it is caring, but is often actually disempowering in reality. Honesty is love. Even although the honesty may be unpalatable it is more loving than lying for approval, fear or protection. Allowing consequences to be felt for harmful behaviour is the kindest most loving thing to offer. The teachings are priceless.

She would patiently listen to my most recent 'drama story' before quietly asking "Were you aware of what you were doing?" I would pause for a minute before confessing, (there was no point in doing anything else) "Well yes, I guess I did know what I was doing and yes, I have done this before." Once she had established that this had happened before, and therefore in her mind there was no excuse, her response was "Well, enjoy your pain." She did not suffer fools gladly and was disinterested in the excuses or explanations we all make for lacking in responsibility. I regarded her as my spiritual mother. Her psychic expertise was exceptionally accurate. Wisdom poured through her voice and words that bore specific meaning were clearly delivered with loving firmness. Wisely she would never make decisions for anyone: she left this task to us.

In one particularly deep reading she informed me that I would reach the font of all knowledge and visit places where I would have to face danger. Her intense blue eyes penetrated in an earnest desire to make me understand something that felt especially important to her, and with a serious expression in her eyes she insisted, "You must remember what I am saying and never forget this. - You must fear nothing. This knowledge will keep you safe when you are in dangerous territory." This information was way above my head at that time and I had no idea what she was talking about. Was I going to a war zone? What danger? Where the heck was the font of all knowledge? Naively thinking this must be a place in Greece or Egypt it was many years later that I came to understand what she meant.

> Fear lives in the mind – it is our imagination creating possibilities from our past (usually painful) experiences. It will feel real but it is not and it can take over our entire lives. When fear has taken over we ask low quality questions that often have no clear answer and causes more anxiety, feeding more fear and keeping us locked in a never-ending perpetual cycle of anxiety. Ask high quality questions that are based on what you know, and that have an answer.

She was to guide me through my life for many more years. This continued even after she died, because she gave me another incredible opportunity to grow leaving explicit instructions that I was to facilitate her funeral service. This was a both an immense honour, but also a painfully difficult thing to do. Even after her death she was offering me yet another teaching experience. The immense and eternal gratitude I will always have for this wonderful lady, who was instrumental in saving and guiding my life with dedicated unconditional love and wisdom, is beyond words.

> The font of all knowledge is the natural source of all wisdom. It is not something we can study intellectually but a wisdom that comes from the soul where we know everything we need to, when we need to know. Ego mind is our barrier to the source of our soul wisdom. The more we think we know, the less we are able to get to know more of the infinite knowledge available to us. The most limiting thing we can say to ourselves is "I know that!"

The vigilant focus on my emotional healing continued to open my heart. Life was slowly but steadily improving. However, I had attached my new awareness, happiness, energy and sense of power to my soul man. He was extremely self-assured and fearlessly held onto his power in most situations. He told me how he injured his knee quite severely and was taken to hospital in an ambulance. Assessing the damage with x-rays, the doctor then informed him he needed emergency surgery. His response to this news was to ask the surgeon how many of these particular surgeries he had performed. The answer came - not many, maybe 2 – 3 a year. This was not sufficient for him to confidently trust and allow the doctor to operate on his knee, so, not prepared to compromise himself, he simply asked for his x-rays, thanked the doctor for his time and went to another hospital where he asked the same question. Here he was told 3-4 a month. Happy with this he went ahead with the surgery. "It's my knee and I have to live with it 24/7, I want someone experienced to look after me this is my life, but the surgeons' job. There is a difference."

His sense of value for himself was powerful. I did not know then, but he was reflecting to me what I needed to access within myself. He was showing me what confidence looked like and what I was building within myself, essential for my life and happiness. **Actually I was becoming more comfortable with myself and although his connection to me helped enormously, my commitment to work on myself played a much bigger part in my healing and happiness than I gave credit for.**

> It is not our usual response to give praise or appreciation to ourselves for our achievements, instead we often dismiss or minimise them as if they are meaningless, when, in actual fact they are a big deal. If we have stepped outside our normal comfort zone, changed or done something that we believed we couldn't do, however small it may appear to be, it is important to acknowledge these events in our lives in order to build our confidence and self-esteem. This is not the same as bragging or desperately looking for attention and approval but a gracious connection to yourself where you are sending yourself a message that you did well and you are recognising your own achievement. In other words, you are being your own best friend in a kind loving and caring way. Minimising these achievements is EGO and equally as destructive to self-esteem as arrogance!

My companions at that time were a group of strong spiritual friends who were wonderfully supportive, many of them interested in several different types of healing work.

When we hung out they constantly encouraged me to become more proactive in healing others, as they were. This was of no interest to me at all. Firstly, my own healing was my priority. Secondly, any confidence in my abilities had not developed, and my insecure ego was running the show persistently whispering in my mind that I was not good enough and everyone was better.

Although I was learning to trust my growing intuition a little more, my insecurity and painfully low self-esteem still blocked me. My enthusiastic friends appeared to see something in me that I did not. They would gently persuade me to channel information that they would try to record. We would check the equipment – "One two, one two, testing, testing over and out" all working great, "Okay let's do it, press record" We sat in silent meditation then the information would start to come and I would speak usually with no clue what was being said. Then excited to hear the recording played back, we sat around the recording equipment and pressed play – out from the machine came loud crackling electrical interference "Swshhhcrrssssshhhh" "What's wrong with it" my friend said. "We tested it, there was nothing wrong before, do it again!" Much to my friends' frustration same thing happened again and again. From my perspective, all of this was just a bit of fun and unlike my friends I did not take it too seriously. But it was definitely useful in building my confidence.

Ego shows up in many forms: insecurity, arrogance it is the same thing. Ego feeds from the stories we create in our minds and the meaning we give to these stories which in turn creates an identity for us. Ego cannot

> really survive in presence, vulnerability - which is
> honesty - and acceptance of what is without adding a
> story to the experience.

My connection with my soul man continued infrequently by phone but when we talked it was open and honest. It was strange situation, as we never seemed to need each other. Knowing we were there wherever we were in the world was enough. The initial finding of each other seemed to be the most important thing for us. In one of our conversations he spoke frankly - "You know, and I know, when we get together and make love, our lives will change forever." His matter-of-fact tone - as if it was already a done deal, freaked me out, but I knew he was right. We had found something life-changing, rare, precious. As he said, we were cut from the same cloth.

I was experiencing new feelings. Some of them were a bit strange so I talked with my spiritual mother about this, asking for help. I'm concerned, something strange is happening that I don't understand, I haven't felt like this before, it feels very weird. As she quietly listened to my description of the new sensations that made no sense, I felt her wisely smiling on the other end of the phone. There was a moment of silence, she then kindly explained "My love, this is what joy feels like." Knowing she was absolutely right, tears of it trickled down my cheeks.

> Happiness is something we can only share with another
> person and not "get" from them. It is the personal
> responsibility of each one of us to take care of our own
> happiness. Giving someone else responsibility and
> credit for our happiness puts that person under pres-

sure and sooner or later they will fail in the impossible task to always make someone else happy.

This is when both parties feel let down and disappointed, then blame each other for the sadness, victimizing everyone. Our own happiness is our own individual responsibility and is achieved by listening, honouring, acknowledging and treating ourselves with the greatest love and respect, taking care and giving ourselves what we need as individuals in each moment. Then, we are able to share our happiness with the people we love.

A few months later I made a trip to France to see my man. Taking a taxi from the airport into the city I chatted with the driver on the way, mentioning that I had driven in Paris a few years before and loved it. Clearly feeling my excitement, the driver jokingly asked if I wanted to drive the taxi. Astonished, but all over it like a rash, my instant and gleeful answer was, "Yes of course!" Within seconds I was behind the wheel of the taxi, manouvering the car up and down the narrow city streets until we eventually pulled up outside my hotel. The poor driver, I'm sure, bitterly regretting his offer to let me anywhere near the steering wheel of his car, prised open his tightly closed eyes, and groaned a welcome sigh of relief. Hey ho, he earned a big tip for the fun!

I checked into my little hotel for the night, had a nice walk, then dinner, and some sightseeing in the vibrant city. He was on a business trip that had been extended until the Saturday morning, this was not an issue for me and I enjoyed my evening. Next morning he called me, saying there was a problem at his house, apparently his basement had flooded and unfortunately we would need to stay in the hotel for the weekend. Mulling over the information, sensing something felt unclear with this, but not really able to dispute it, **I consciously chose to ignore it**.

This was the first time a small niggling doubt had risen and trickled into my heart as far as he was concerned, but it was unmistakable and was not to be the last time. But for now we were in Paris having fun, the flooded basement story now filed in a far distant corner at the back of my mind, ignored for the time being, but not forgotten.

> **When something is real and true it feels peaceful and there are no questions or any doubt, even if unpalatable it is easier to accept than a lie or a half-truth. We do not always recognize an untruth for a number of reasons. The person delivering it may be very convincing or we want to believe the story because it fits with our desires or needs to hold onto something.**
>
> **If this is associated with a love relationship we will accept stories easily especially if we do not have a high level of self-esteem. This drives us onto the road of denial. An untruth is not necessarily a deliberate lie but is a version of truth, normally used to protect the person telling it because of their fear of being hurt. There are different versions of untruths – vagueness, lying by omission, leaving out parts of the whole picture, implying or bending the truth. None are honest and those listening will know this on a deep level, as they will always have a question or doubt in their heart. Our heart hears what our mind often ignores.**

When you add or take away from the truth you are no longer telling the truth. Old beliefs and stories that we are not good enough create a need to protect ourselves and it becomes easy for us to invent believable tales that may be versions or elaborations of the truth. We are not necessarily liars but we can lie in any one moment to protect ourselves, for our own reasons. If this way of communicating continues it has the power to destroy relationships as trust is eroded with every deception, and the very thing we are afraid of, that we will be hurt, is manifested.

When something is not fully true the energy is less peaceful and we ask a lot of questions as we search for a deeper version to what we are hearing. Of course this is an answer in itself. The more we heal and become whole within ourselves the more able we are to handle deeper truth. When we are broken and insecure we will run and deny any honesty because our ego has taken over to protect us and will not allow us to face possible hurt again. Fantasy in the form of denial becomes the game we play. To build confidence as individuals we must learn to listen and trust our own truth. Following someone else's truth can bring us to deep sorrow and sadness. This lesson, I was to discover later...

We had a wonderful weekend and the following week he called and we talked about the excellent time we shared, both of us agreeing how much fun we had. Then he said we would need to do this at his pace, he wasn't going anywhere, but I would need to be patient. Of course I agreed because I loved him and although my relationship with myself was improving, I was more focused on him, accommodating his wishes almost every time. I loved him a lot more than I loved myself, a lot more. Love must come from within ourselves, otherwise need takes over and causes pain. I was still to learn this at another stage of my growth.

> Making allowances, accommodating too readily, especially when our inner voice is whispering the truth, is an indication of lack of self-love. When we are lacking love within ourselves we need and search for love from outside. This causes pain, neediness and stress, especially at times when it is not given in the way we want it, and we can easily fall into co-dependency and anxiety, then love becomes conditional, then the power and control games begin.
>
> Love does not cause pain when unconditional. It is simply love and results in building more love. Unconditional love is grown and strengthened by our inner self-love and our healthy relationship within. Need is what causes us pain. Co-dependent love or conditional love is grown through our fears, lack of self-esteem and protection from hurt, which in turn creates power struggles and control issues within our relationships and blocking unconditional love from developing.

As my transformational awakening process continued, my trust in my insight developed more. My first client arrived unplanned and unexpectedly while in the hair salon having my hair done. While cutting my hair my hairdresser was chatting about her need to make some changes in her life. One of them was her desire to develop her skills as a hairdresser. She had been in the same salon for nine years and wanted to move but hadn't found the confidence to take the step. There were also some personal things that were troubling her and she felt stuck. She was aware that I was practising energy work, and I suggested that we had a session to see if it would help. Of course there was no fee, as she would be doing me a favour. She was happy to try, and we made a date for transformation healing session. This was a first for us both, and an opportunity to practice with no expectations or pressure from either of us. Truthfully, when she left after her session, I had no clue if it had helped her or not and completely let it go. Six weeks later, when I called the salon to book another hair appointment, she was no longer there. It seemed she had moved to another salon, and was now engaged to be married, and starting a new life. Okay, something was working!

Soon more people came. From where, I don't know. Somehow the word spread. Before long with no advertising, flyers, brochures or even business cards, what I never expected had begun: I was working with others and healing was happening. To be honest it never felt like I was doing anything except getting out of the way to allow the energy to come through. 'It' was doing me.

> The vibration of this work is attractive to those who are ready, so marketing and advertising in the traditional way was therefore not necessary.

It came to the point where I had so many clients that my job as a sales rep really needed to go. This was a big step. Although I was busy, resigning and giving up my monthly pay cheque to rely on my own ability to pay my bills, triggered my insecurity big time. Needing to feel safer with this decision, I decided that once I regularly brought in enough to pay the bills from my healing work, I would let go of my job. Within three months it was clear that financially I would be fine and could leave. Wow this is powerful stuff! Soon I was so busy with individual clients that I took the next step, which was to work with groups. This was another first and nerve-racking.

I facilitated my first group on a Wednesday evening in my own house. To my surprise around twenty-five people showed up, and it was then that I realised this was the way forward. The power of the group work was obvious right from the beginning and this way of working with people became my preference.

> When making any big life changes, it is important and wise to create safety as without it we can become stuck in situations that do not fulfil us. Without safety we can mentally and emotionally wobble and give up. Fear and excitement are opposite sides of the same energy. When fear is great we get stuck and never experience the excitement from breaking through to the other side and into excitement. There is a fine line in being stuck in fear and taking the necessary steps to move our lives forward outside of our often limiting comfort zones. The wise way is to create safety, with small baby steps. Working with what we know, and not on what we don't know, will move us forward to eventually bring us to our full potential. We will often only find out what the next baby step is once we have taken the first.

My next step was to put my house on the market for sale and at the same time, little by little, I slowly let go of all of my possessions. Many people thought I was crazy for giving up a steady job, company car, expense account and all the trappings and apparent security of corporate life, for this 'new age wacky stuff.' For me personally it simply felt right. By now trusting myself, and my spiritual guidance more than ever before. Considering the life I was living only three short years ago, and how little trust or belief in myself I had, this was quite a massive leap.

> It didn't mean I was free from fear, but fear no longer controlled me. Moments of fear will always show up when we step into unknown territory. We can intensify fear with imaginary stories that we create in our minds or we can stay focused on the present moment where we access our point of power in the moment. Faith and connection to divine power, which is greater than any fear, gave me strength to let go and move forward in slow but steady steps.

When I finally resigned from my company, they asked me to continue working until they found a suitable replacement. I was flexible and happily agreed – it was of no concern to me how long this took. Astonishingly my last working day as an employee was the precise day my house was sold. All on the one day my home, job and company car were gone. It could not have been planned better. Life was certainly changing quickly, the whole transition was a very big deal and one I wasn't taking lightly. By this point I owned very little in terms of material possessions: my clothes, the music CDs I used in my sessions and workshops, a small box of books and small items were all I had left – everything else given away or sold. Now it was up to me. It was a wonderful feeling to be free from all the trappings of materialistic living. Trust was my new mantra. My life indeed had changed completely.

> Letting go of "stuff" offers an immense feeling of freedom. Attaching to stuff, people, situations, in fact anything, creates the opposite of freedom! It is not the things that are the issue but our attachment to them.

A far cry from my previous existence, my life became an adventure. I relocated to the north of Scotland, basing myself there while at the same time following the energy and guidance with complete trust. I travelled around Europe, bringing workshops to Germany, Spain, France and Slovenia. People came with all sorts of issues, but also simply to be in the energy field and to develop and grow through deeper connection. As they learned to listen, connect and trust their own personal truth, they found more inner peace, more emotional freedom and confidence, at the same time healing old emotional traumas, letting go of limiting beliefs, to free their lives and realise their true potential.

My role as facilitator was to create a safe and sacred space to support emotional healing by listening and following the vibrational energy trail back to the source of trauma and fragmentation and connecting. By getting myself, and my filtered mindsets out of the way by invoking and calling in Universal Energies I basically become a conduit for the consciousness to work through. In the early years the focus at workshops was predominately letting go of old pain. This important work is very a necessary part of the healing process but it is only part of the process: the bigger part of healing is to the connection.

Unfortunately, it was soon very apparent that people were becoming hooked on the releasing process, and were not connecting or taking responsible actions to make the changes to what they could to improve their lives. My intention was, and still is to empower individuals and not to create followers. With this realisation, I decided to spend more time breaking down the conceptual understandings and literal comprehensions that people had about healing, spirituality, energy work, the super natural and mysticism. Healing through connection bringing the concepts into reality, and the physical world.

Everything in our real life experiences, every thought, action, word spoken, either connects or disconnects us. Until we are connected we will continue with the same old mindsets and patterns that hold us stuck, going around in circles. As we connect to fragmentation we become more whole, and are able to see more and more of the bigger life picture.

Ego looks for the supernatural and the extra-ordinary events to feel special. We already are special and important but our ego needs more and more reassurance. With openness and humbleness we can see that ordinary everyday life experiences are our opportunities to bring extraordinary miracles into our life and similarly natural everyday simple things are the supernatural. It is not the other way around. Strong spiritual ego needs the extraordinary and supernatural to feel satisfied, everyday ordinary life is where it all happens!

Although each of my seminars has the same intention, to empower, let go and heal pain that is often buried deep into our cellular memory for years, free minds, open hearts, and create consciousness awareness, not one of workshop is remotely like another. Each day of every workshop is a blank canvas created and cultured on that day. Participants may attend seminars regularly, but they always have a completely new and different experience each time. There is no schedule or agenda. The sacred space is opened with a clear, focused intention to heal and connect to deeper love, then listening, reading and interpreting the energy, allows the healing to unfold in the moment. It is a powerful and wonderful experience of truly connecting to living in the moment.

*

My next move was to a small rented maison de village in a tiny village nestled in the vineyards of Provence in the South of France. My move to this beautiful part of the world happened easily and was a wonderfully mystical experience.

After I had given away all of my possessions a few years previously my life had become quite nomadic, then one birthday, someone gave me a beautiful cup and saucer as a birthday present. Happily admiring and appreciating the lovely gift, I heard myself say, "I think it's time to get a house to go with this".

A few days later while facilitating a seminar in Scotland while in the alchemical vibration of the seminar, I set my intention to build a new home. How and when it would happen was still unknown to me. The only clarity I had at that point was that I was ready for my own home again and

I wanted that home to be in the South of France, somewhere not quite on the coast but further inland.

A French woman who lived in Scotland was attending this particular seminar, so during a break I had a conversation with her and arranged to have conversational French lessons. In the same seminar an American lady, also participating in the group, informed me that she had a good friend who lived in Provence in the South of France, whose intention was to move to New Zealand in a few months time. She wondered if I would like her to talk to her friend about my intention to move, as it may be beneficial for both of us? Would I? Of course, I agreed without a moment's hesitation.

The next day an email arrived from the lady in Provence describing her house. She was renting from her French landlady who curiously had a Scottish Grandmother and if I were interested in taking it further, she would be delighted to speak to me about leasing the property. Before even seeing a picture of what was to become my new home, I knew it would be perfect for me. Within three months I was moved in. Having nothing to move except my clothes, CDs and books. It was easy, but once there, I set about buying the things I needed to make a home for myself again.

Manifesting dreams into reality requires clear, specific and focused intention as to whatever your desire may be. All possible effort then has to be made to align with your intention. Divine grace will then come through to support the creation of your desire. There is no such thing as handing anything over and letting the "Universe" provide, we have to make it happen and meet the universe at least half way if not more. Creating our lives requires effort and responsibility.

My nurturing home in France was now a perfect place to regroup and restore my energy. This was essential as the intensity of my workshops often drained me, and because of my love and passion for my work, I often forgot the importance of looking after my own energy. Regular, rest, regrouping and filling myself up was crucial.

About a year later an opportunity to move to North America arrived and my life began to move in an entirely different direction. Before I even knew Canada was to be part of my agenda. While window-shopping in town I found myself outside a sports shop, looking at a pair of very expensive walking boots for sale. Waterproof, weatherproof, everything-proof, full meal deal winter hiking boots. This was strangely significant only because hiking is not my thing, therefore it made little sense, but without too much thought I was inside the store to try them on and while I was at it I asked the assistant to show me some super duper thick, warm woollen socks to go with them. Leaving the shop with a lot less cash in my purse but happily carrying my new boots and socks, I asked myself what the heck was going on now and what was the reason for my unusual purchases?

Deciding it was okay, I could always return them tomorrow I thought, "I'll sleep on it and see how it feels." Then, I headed for home. Still pondering my purchases I checked my email once in the house and more pieces of the puzzle fell into place. There in my email inbox was an invitation to go to Canada, ticket paid, place to stay, the only thing required from me, was to show up. I sat there stunned once again staring at the email. "Oooohhh! Now it makes sense, that's why I need the boots!" It was November and winter had already arrived in Canada. There is always a bigger picture.

> Listening to guidance can be challenging as often we are guided to take actions that make no logical sense. It is important to recognise the moments when we listen to the guidance and follow it even though we do not have all the pieces of the puzzle. Living spiritually means having faith in the guidance, which comes from a deeper connection than our logical minds can understand.

On this first trip I was to meet the woman who was to become my future business partner and who I came to regard as my best friend. We shared a similar philosophy regarding healing, though with completely different gifts and abilities. We understood that by working holistically with the mental, emotional, physical and spiritual aspects of a person, in addition to making connections and by supporting the body's innate intelligence, healing begins. This has the potential to create wellness even although there may be a labelled diagnosis of sickness as I myself had with diabetes.

My experience of living in Canada was a combination of amazing, life changing, crazy, terrible adventures and became another unexpected and richly profound teaching on many levels. While there I added to my natural healing ability by training in craniosacral therapy, reiki, stress and wellness consulting, and breath work technique, somato respiratory integration. However, my clients found it more effective when I brought in my natural intuitive capabilities to connect to the source of their pain. In addition to more "traditional training" I continued with my own personal development by frequent attendance to many more workshops in the US, Europe and Canada.

Even although we may have been diagnosed and labelled with a chronic illness, wellness can still be achieved. One of the keys is to not take on the label and become a patient, instead continue your connection to be an individual person.

This can be challenging as once the label is given we are treated as that label and not as the person. We can easily lose ourselves and become identified with that label. As a person who has diabetes I chose never to take it on and embody it. I deal with the diabetes as part of who I am, but I do not fight it or revolve my life around it. I also do not handover the control to the doctors, who well intentioned will sometimes assume power and control over it, victimising me unnecessarily. This is my life, my body and that makes me responsible, no-one else.

Our mental attitude is crucial to our wellbeing. A positive attitude has the ability to keep us re-enforcing wellness, instead of allowing illness to take charge of us. What we focus on expands. Focusing on sickness and what can go wrong can create more sickness as everything then is decided from fear. On the other hand when we focus on wellness and our well being we give ourselves a better chance to improve our situation.

My future business partner had just moved into a new office and her dream was to create an eclectic strip full of shops and offices for all types of holistic therapies. This was not my vision at all, but I drifted into this illusion with her, as it seemed to fit at the time.

After a few of years of travelling back and forward between Europe and Canada I gained residency and was helping to run the office, often working on reception before my client base built. This set the stage for an entangled and imbalanced working situation, as my unique abilities unintentionally slipped under the radar, and I along with them.

The idea to create a holistic and educational centre for awareness and healing seemed like a logical proposition at the time, however the moment I signed the business contract, heaviness descended into my heart. I spoke of my misgivings and concerns on how I felt, but was convinced it was the best for both of us and I chose to file it away.

> Well-intentioned help is often heavily disguised manipulations. When we listen to our gut instinct but decide to ignore it and not take action, it is a recipe for disaster.

We became very busy working with people on all levels. When everything else had failed, traditional or alternative, people came to our office. My partner would call me into her room where her client lay face down on the therapy table. Without knowing anything about them, sometimes, not even their name, I would tune in, by holding their feet for a few seconds to connect to their emotional energy field. Reading their energy and following the trail back to the source of their problem, I was then able to translate what I was picking up into understandable language.

One lady came in to the office suffering with chronic pain since her car accident four years earlier. She was unable to work, drive, do her shopping and could not move or turn her head due to severe pain and had tried everything to help her situation including, Physiotherapy, Psychology, massage, Occupational Health therapy, Chiropractic, Psychiatry – she had been everywhere but was not getting better. As many people did, she came to me as a last resort.

She sat on a chair opposite me as I tuned into her, it became clear to me that she was depressed, disconnected, fragmented and in a lot of physical pain, although it appeared that the physical pain was no longer connected directly to the accident, but from her emotional distress.

I asked her to close her eyes then began to guide her through a reconnection process. By connecting to her deeper truth this would increase her strength and bring more ease to her system. After twenty minutes she was solidly connected, had acknowledged and validated her individual soul experience. Then with a surprised look, she turned her head from right to the left, then up and down, her eyes big and bright as they filled with grateful tears, she gasped, "I have no pain, I can move, it's unbelievable, I have no pain."

As soon as she made the connection, a new energy flooded her whole system allowing her chronic pain to dissipate and peace settle instead. After her initial session she went from strength to strength, and soon was able to go back to work, drive, and live a normal life again. Her Occupational Therapist contacted me to discuss what happened, as it had clearly been so helpful to her client. She wanted to come in and see how it was done, what I did and what was the name of my therapy?

It was challenging to try and explain that the communication with the client was on another level entirely. Engaging energetically with her soul and not her conditioned mind to help her to connect with her deeper truth was possibly something that would not make sense to anyone else but her. I made an attempt to make it clear that this is an individual experience, and watching what I was doing would not make too much logical sense.

Explaining my work has always been a problem and when some enquiring and interested soul asked, "So what is it you do?" I would always draw a blank. I was truly unable to answer clearly in words that made logical sense. Working with energy and connecting and communicating on a soul level is a completely unique experience for every individual and cannot be understood logically, rationally and is an exceptional occurrence that has exclusive meaning only to the person involved.

> "For those who understand no explanation is necessary, and for those who do not understand, no explanation is enough." – Thomas Aquinas

> My work cannot be described as a "technique" but a combination of factors has created the potent healing sessions experienced by my clients. These include a natural clarity, insight and intuitive ability enhanced by the many years of the deep cleansing processes I put myself through, along with the willingness to do whatever it takes: but because it's completely natural, and therefore simple for me, it is quite challenging to explain.

> Seriously, as far as I was concerned it felt like just another day at the office! This, of course was not the

case and many people experienced what can only be described as incredible and even miraculous shifts in their mental, emotional and physical states.

However, because of my own inability to properly articulate and acknowledge my work, it resulted in subtly minimising myself for many years, and eventually this was to create an energetic disaster of gargantuan proportions - there were still more big lessons to learn. Nowadays when asked to describe my work, my answer is simple - I follow the energy trail back to source, back to the root of the problem, no matter what that problem may be. Once connected to the source the symptoms dissipate and healing can begin.

Word spread throughout the city as more and more people recommended their friends and family members. My business partner had an amazing ability to change and redirect tension patterns in the physical bodies of clients and miracles often happened as pain and problems disappeared under her care.

My work with the emotional, mental, spiritual patterns worked in conjunction, and our clients accessed healing potential on all levels. We became a formidable team treating people holistically. As things developed over time, people with all manner of issues arrived through the office door, including addictions, bereavement and loss, relationship problems, confidence and low self esteem, anxiety and behavior problems.

Although now, seeing many people on an individual basis, my true passion was my Core Transformation Seminars.

These life altering, powerful experiential healing workshops involved unexpected healing opportunities that were sometimes indescribable.

Not long after I first arrived in Canada two weekends of Core Transformation Workshops were planned. The registrations were more than anticipated, so the venue was moved from the office to a resources library in a Secondary School. On arrival the energy of the room was dense and heavy, when anyone spoke it was as if they were talking through layers of thick glass sounding muffled and tinny.

After our usual music meditations, invocations, prayers of intention and protection, the energy in the room suddenly cleared and shifted feeling easier and lighter. On the Monday after the first weekend when the staff came into the school they commented that they noticed a change and asked what had been happening in the school over the weekend. They also noticed a marked change in the behaviour of the pupils who appeared calmer and more focused.

The healing vibration affected everyone and everything. One particular lady had showed up for an afternoon session that same weekend. She had recently suffered over sixty seizures within a few weeks. Unable to drive or work, she came to the Core Transformation Seminar not knowing what to expect, nervous, depressed and desperate. As the energy came through she suddenly felt a popping sensation in her ear. Focusing on her I held my hand towards her ear and asked her to open herself to more – "as much as she could handle." She screeched. "Owwwwwchhh this hurts!" The popping increased for around 1–2 minutes, as she groaned with the pain.

Suddenly everything stopped and she became quiet. She looked at me surprised as a smile of delight shone on her face. "I feel different, I do not know what has just happened but something is better." Within a few weeks she was back at work and was able to re-sit her driving test. She was on her way to having her life back.

There are countless examples of these types of experiences. For a number of years I had the honor of working with Innu and Inuit first nations people of Labrador, facilitating Healing Weekends. These were wonderful and humbling experiences where I learned a great deal about faith and vulnerability. I was welcomed into their culture with the utmost love and respect and I am forever grateful for the opportunity I was given.

> **Connection to the source heals, but it is not always apparently obvious what or where the source is.**

Healing happens often when we least expect it and occasionally without intention, but if the opportunity arrives and people are open, changes can occur. I was Skyping with a very wonderful friend of mine when an opportunity came. She was using her old laptop without a camera so I couldn't see her but she could see me. We talked a little then I mentioned that she sounded a bit down and not her usual happy self. She told me she was worried and was scheduled for a biopsy because she had found a large lump on her neck. She had just had an ultrasound that day and she was obviously concerned. While she talked, I tuned in and my hand automatically went to my own neck. She watched my hand move to the exact spot where her lump was and blurted out - "How do you know where my lump is, you are right on the spot?"

Focusing, I suddenly had a flash of her sister. "What's going on with you and your sister?" I asked. She had been having a few difficult conversations with her and often felt tense around her. There seemed to be a power struggle between them. Tuning in more, an unraveling of old resentments and control issues began and more connections were made as we followed the energy trail. Suddenly something felt peaceful and settled and we ended the conversation. Two days later she could no longer find the lump and when she attended for the scheduled biopsy a couple of weeks later, it confirmed there was no longer any lump to biopsy.

These types of experiences happen consistently and regularly. I do not begin to try to understand what is happening and there is no way I can explain them, but I do know that over the years, they happen time and time again. Physical symptoms disappear when emotional connections are made and spiritual growth happens as a consequence. People override and stuff down emotions that they cannot cope with and this can eventually cause pain and sickness on a physical level.

The wealth of experience gained from my time in Canada was incredible with my focus mainly on work, which was my entire passion. When I was working, it actually didn't even feel like work. This was good for everyone but eventually not so much for me.

As the years passed, work began to consume my entire life. Soon working sixteen-hour days, seven days a week became normal. Clearly a major imbalance had developed and I was in dangerous territory. When people asked me where I lived, my answer was Scotland, I work in Canada, but I don't live here. It was true I really didn't have a life and certainly felt I had lost control of my own life! Now sharing a house with my business partner, it got to the point that by the end of the working day, exhausted, barely able to speak, I would drag myself in through the door, kicking off my shoes and stripping out of my clothes as I went along the hallway to my bedroom, closing my door before falling into a dreamless coma.

Drained and shattered, I desperately needed space to regroup but there never seemed to be any. The healing centre was no longer a place of healing for me, I became normalised to an imbalanced lifestyle that did not work and I had completely lost myself, becoming sick and unhappy. I was making the fundamental mistake of not listening to myself, something that I had taught people for years, but was ignoring and now I was living outside of my own truth. For years before I actually left, I knew I needed to go but just couldn't see how. I felt stuck. My loyalty to my friendship with my business partner, my clients and to the healing centre was my priority but any loyalty for myself had disappeared. My capacity to continue working, teaching, facilitating, and speaking was not in doubt, but part of me that was not fully connected was.

> **Having loyalty to others is a noble quality, but unwise if it comes at the expense of your own wellbeing.**

To replenish my energy I would leave to go on holiday to somewhere hot and sunny, or come home to Scotland to spend with my family and soul man, it didn't really matter where I visited, the point was, I had to leave to regain my energy. Something was draining me energetically to absolute depletion. There were clearly habits that had re-established themselves that I wasn't seeing.

After two or three weeks of rest I felt and looked human again but often while I was driving to the airport on the day I was to return, I found myself unable to stop the tears from streaming down my face, sobbing for the entire journey as sadness engulfed me. BIG CLUE!

All the signs were there but I was unable to see a way out my misplaced loyalties had become more important than my health, wealth and happiness. I was educating my clients on how to love themselves and I was not fully applying it to myself. My ego prevented me from seeing what was sticking out like a sore thumb and I had dropped the ball on the fundamental principal of loving yourself, making excuses, explaining, justifying why I couldn't change things around to bring back more balance. Eventually something would have to give.

We can easily be swept enthusiastically along onto another's path when the energy of the other person merges with our own. We easily can lose the ability to distinguish who is in control, us or the other individual, and also if we are following our own true path or theirs.

We will find ourselves going with the flow, even telling ourselves that's what we are doing. Actually we are bobbing around in another persons flow, and not directing our own and eventually will become lost. Unfortunately we can also drown in another's flow, disappearing and sinking below the surface. It is more challenging to identify this dynamic if both parties appear to want the same thing as how this end goal is created may need to be done in entirely different ways for the sake of each individual's wellbeing.

> Creating, directing and BEING our own flow, while allowing others to direct theirs, while we merge on the occasions when it works for both parties, keeps us safe, and allows our creative energy to build, and prevents us from losing sight of our own dreams and desires. I was eventually to discover how incredibly important this lesson is for success.

On one of my trips home my man came to visit it would be months between us meeting but when we met it was effortless and easy. We just hung out and enjoyed each other's company. I really needed these times as it brought balance into my stressful life. We seemed like we were a pair of old slippers, comfortable and cosy. It suited us both in our busy lives. I trusted him, letting him into my world on every level. He was not too open but claimed to be working on it. I believed him. I was in love and he was telling me how he loved me too. He often commented on how naïve I was to trust my business partner so openly - interestingly she said the same about him. I simply trusted them both - with my life – Yep I was naïve!

> Blindly trusting another person however much we love them is naïve and even unsafe. We must constantly listen to ourselves first in order to trust ourselves before placing trust in another. This is simple wisdom.

When I met him at the airport, he looked at me and immediately recognised I was stressed. "What's up?" he asked looking at me knowing something was wrong. "Nothing I'm fine" the classic bog standard BS response that people in denial give. I'M FINE! Not pushing me or arguing the point, instead he asked if I wanted to have lunch. "Hmmm not sure do you?" He looked at me strangely and slightly irritated said "Yes that's why I'm asking you."

We drove a little distance and stopped in a small town. "Where do you want to go?" he asked. My response was similar to before "Hmm not sure. Where do you want to go?" I heard him take a deep breath trying to be patient "I don't know, I've never been here before, you know this town, you choose." "Okay let's go in there" I pointed towards the first place in sight, not really paying attention but not wanting to make the decision.

It wasn't over yet. We sat down to look at our menus. "What are you having?" he said looking over the top of his menu. "Hmm not sure what are you having?" I asked. That was it he'd had enough. "Stop it" he said. "Stop what?" I asked, shocked at his frustrated tone. "I am asking you a question because I value your opinion and you are answering me with another question. You are giving me your power and I don't want it. Stop it."

He may as well have thrown a bucket of ice-cold water over me. I had no idea that I had gone into the habit of not taking responsibility for decisions. I also realised I was doing the same thing with my business partner: she made all the decisions, and although they were discussed nothing was done unless she decided. I felt powerless and not in control of my life and this had happened very subtly over time - what a wake-up call! Thank goodness he had called me on it, now I could reverse what I was doing. Another major life lesson, I saw that this was one way I was weakening my energy. To this day I have a lot to thank him for.

Our vital energy can be depleted in numerous ways but some of these are not always obvious. Our unconscious habits, environment, people, food, drink, noise, electric lighting, to name but a few. Some of these we are unable to control but what we can control is our habits, who we hang around with and what we eat and drink. The problem is identifying what weakens us and what strengthens us. Sensitive people often have a hard time in environments that are full of electronics and overhead lighting.

Every time I was asked a question, I replied with another question instead of taking responsibility and answering honestly I was skilfully deflecting the question and at the same time unconsciously giving away my power. As I objectively looked at this, it was exactly what I was doing with my business partner. What we do in one thing we do in everything! Even although I was teaching others about how easy it is to become disempowered, I had fallen into the very common trap myself. The habit I had unconsciously developed was unknowingly disempowering me. One of the exercises I give people to do is to make conscious decision of value for themselves, if we do not make decisions for ourselves there are plenty of people who will be happy to make them for us and at the same time will enjoy the power this gives them.

My time in Canada continued but as the years passed, I often yearned to come home. I felt trapped. Work intensified, and there seemed to be more and more projects constantly being brought to the table. Often there were three big projects on the go at the same time, regularly with a new one starting before the one before was completed. Under the intense pressure, my blood pressure shot through the roof, I was getting sick and desperately needed to change my lifestyle in major ways. At this stage as a person with long term diabetes who had avoided the normal "cocktail" of blood pressure, cholesterol and diuretics drugs often given to people with my condition, which can have devastating and can have terrible side effects that I had no intention of suffering from, meant I had to act fast. I made drastic changes, to my diet and workload. I stepped back when possible and refused to bend to the relentless pressure.

> **Too much external stress and pressure will cause internal stress on the body and will create sickness. It is our individual responsibility to listen to this.**

The thing that I loved doing the most - my workshops - suffered, I had no energy left to facilitate and had to cancel those that were scheduled, feeling it unfair and disrespectful to both myself and the participants knowing I could not give them the best I knew I was capable of giving.

My eldest daughter came for a visit and helped me see how little control I had in the running of the business. Things had to change and they did!

The ending came, not unexpectedly, but nevertheless was appalling and traumatic, as if an explosion of unfathomable magnitude had erupted, shattering my life into a million minute particles and bringing that chapter to a sudden and devastating end. Everything happened at the same time. It was another major wake up call.

The last year in Canada was one of the most painful years of my life to date. I developed pneumonia at the start of the year, which took me months to recover from. Just as my health was improving I heard the shocking news that my spiritual mother had passed away suddenly with a massive heart attack. At the same time my soul man dropped off the radar and became unavailable. He was going through something important for him. Not wanting support in these situations, his typical way was to withdraw from the world, and from me.

My business partner, who I regarded as my best friend or sister, seemed to have morphed into a stranger overnight, and I no longer had any ability to connect with her. She had gone on a trip, fallen in love while there. I was very happy for her but also to be honest, selfishly saw it as an opportunity to transition my life. Now with someone else she had support and I felt I could leave. Finding it difficult to connect we decided to go to the house where the seminars were held to spend a few days together as we tried to resolve or situation. There it became even more obvious that there was no going forward as business partners or even friends. We discussed me going back to the UK to base myself there Ideally I wanted to stay connected with the centre making the transition over a six-month period, organising things to keep the center running. I would come back, quarterly, to work.

This was not to be. Her new relationship seemed to be her main priority. Exciting and all consuming, she was on another path and appeared to want me completely out of her life. I had to accept that I could no longer reach her. In one deep discussion, now realising we both needed to be free to move on, I said "I release myself from any written, verbal, spiritual or soul contracts with you." The deal was done on all levels apart from the physical which is always the last and easiest to resolve. Then, on a private visit to our accountant he advised me to get out. The back end of the business had been poorly constructed and for me a financially disastrous mess. My accountant's shocking advice to let my business go, and to accept that after thirteen years of blood, sweat and tears, I would leave only with my experience, was a massive blow, quite literally demolishing my world into dust. My life in Canada was clearly over. Within one month everything fell apart and with none of my usual network of support around me, I did too.

Looking back, it had to happen and was way overdue. I was being given the gift of a gigantic spiritual boot up the ass. I had no option but to let go: it was taken out of my hands.

I came home on my knees, drained energetically on all levels: emotionally, financially, mentally, physically, I was sick and broken. The consequence of being loyal to everything and everyone without including myself was heartbreaking. Thankfully the wakeup call forced me to look at my part in the whole situation. I had to quite literally pull myself back together from the shattering experience I had just gone through.

I needed help so I reached out to some of my trusted, beautiful clients. They willing became my support system saying they were happy to give back some of the help they had received over the years. I was the one who everyone came to for help and guidance, but now I needed help, and all I had to do was ask and it happened, My true friends came forward with their open hearts and held me up.

Vulnerability is emotional honesty in the present moment. Vulnerability is viewed as weakness if seen through the judgment of ego, which is always seeking power in one form or another. Ego sees vulnerability as an opportunity to take power and to control another person. Vulnerability viewed from compassion and love has huge power and strength to open hearts and generate more love, solidly building the power of love and becomes an immensely humbling and potent energy experience to be practiced with wisdom. Be wise with the people whom you are vulnerable with as some will exploit to take power and control over you. Insecurity is also ego!

As this whole process unfolded it was a great experience to see egos at play, mine and others, and another reality check. My vulnerable state was apparent and some people judged this as weakness. There were also one or two who tried to take advantage of the opportunity and assume power, not their own. But mine. They stepped forward offering to help, as 'Greeks baring Gifts' cleverly hiding their own agendas and desire for power and control. In my fragile, weakened and insecure state, on a couple of occasions, I was taken in, but as my healing process continued, my strength and clarity returned and their true intentions became very apparent. Soon they were no longer in my life - I was broken but not dead!

We all need time and space and it is important to give yourself the time it takes that you as an individual need. But, use the time to work with yourself, without

> wallowing. It is easy to step back and do nothing and fill the space you have created with pain and negativity caught up in the painful story. Using the time to heal means you work with yourself to see the part you played and what you have learned as well as nourishing yourself with love and compassion. Working in this way we come through the other side stronger and see the gifts we have received in the process. Withdrawing and wallowing is not the same thing.

They say that time heals and it does. By giving myself some desperately needed attention, my energy levels slowly increased and the brokenness mended. Listening to what was essential for my own wellbeing and giving myself exactly that, whether it was rest, food, sunshine, sleep, or doing tasks without adding pressure, l became my own loyal best friend. After some months my strength returned and I began to see a light at the end of the tunnel, or to be more precise, slowly and dimly at first, became the light in the tunnel.

> Coming out of the other side of yet another humbling trauma, I became emotionally clearer and stronger and gave consideration to myself on a level that was deeper than ever before. I found my experience brought me much more clarity and kindness, understanding and compassion than before. Once again I was walking the walk, applying the philosophy of conscious awareness to myself in my day to day life. When I was slapbang in the middle of the whole painful circumstance I would say, "I would not wish this on my worst enemy," but the experience helped me to grow in a profound way, bringing me

to a humbler place than ever before. The crucial teaching of listening and loving myself, strengthened and empowered with compassion, resulted with my healing work developing onto a deeper level than before.

A few years before I had returned from Canada my man and I had talked about creating a home base together. We both travelled extensively but we agreed we could make it work and that it was a good idea but I needed to look at what I would do with living and working in Canada. He planned and analysed everything, every point thought through in minute detail, but when the topic of a life together came up – he had nothing, other things were more important and it was given no real attention. Looking back, I believe he was searching for excuses and was terrified of making any form of true commitment. It was to be the beginning of yet another ending, but at that stage, ending was not what I wanted. I was in love.

Back in UK I was able to see more clearly how work dominated his life, creeping into his weekends - every weekend. We planned a mini trip to get a break and some sun. "I am going to make this happen" he assured me when I questioned his extreme workload. Then two weeks before we were due to go he called "It's not going to happen, why don't you go on your own and I'll try to join you?" I was driving my car at the time and almost ran off the road. "I am so angry right now I will have to go" I was livid, I couldn't speak I was so let down, hurt and angry. But what did I do? I made my peace and went on my own anyway, but it seemed relatively easy for him to disappoint me. I knew I needed the break so I took it. I didn't need him to come with me but I did want him to come. That was the difference.

> Wanting someone in your life and needing someone are two different things. Needing someone comes from a place of dependency and need. Wanting someone comes from the strength of knowing what you want and knowing whom you want to share your time with.

Being geographically closer I became far more aware of vagueness and secrecy. Some things just did not make sense or add up. I heard a lot of excuses or what certainly felt like excuses, that I couldn't quite put my finger on and therefore could not dispute, but the lack of transparency and energy of what I was feeling didn't match with the words I was hearing. There seemed to be a major fear of intimacy and the closer and easier for us to be together, the more stressed and anxious he seemed to become. He seemed anxious of everything that was outside of his control. He often stated proudly that he took nothing from me, apparently completely unaware that he had my heart almost from the moment we met. When I asked if he trusted me he said yes, but followed with, "But I do not trust myself." Cleary, if this was the case, **it was unsafe for me to leave my heart in his hands.**

> Trust yourself enough to know when it is safe to trust another. Of course people are trustworthy but they are also human and this means they may sometimes be going through situations that can distract them and create confusion or conflict within them. This does not necessarily make them untrustworthy but it may in the moment. It is our responsibility to pick this up, otherwise

we may be placing our life into the hands of someone who in the moment will not be worthy of our trust. We must trust ourselves first

Deliberately not taking from an intimate partner is an unconscious way to avoid commitment. On one level this seems respectful, but it is on a surface level. It can also hide another agenda – it is justifying not giving to the relationship because of not taking. This subtle game prevents the openness, intimacy and vulnerability necessary to nourish a healthy loving relationship and an effective way of self-protection necessary because of fear of intimacy.

Truth always feels peaceful even if the truth is unpalatable. Half-truth, vagueness, lying by omission, lack of transparency, all variations of untruths and cause doubt and suspicion to grow. These habits also effectively erode the basic corner stone and vital component for any healthy relationship to build – Trust. Without trust the relationship becomes a game and power struggles, which eventually can break hearts and destroy love.

By now, we had known each other for sixteen years although for most of this time we had lived on opposite continents. I had no doubt that I loved this man deeply. Now we were living on the same side of the world, I could see the reality more clearly and I realised that for me something wasn't right. I **continued to observe myself in this dynamic for over a year, paying close attention to how it felt in my heart. But I noticed my heart was heavy far to much of the time for me**

to be happy and healthy. I still wanted to create the home we had agreed to build years previously, but whenever we discussed moving forward, he expertly convinced me that we were, albeit at a glacial pace. He constantly told me we were okay and everything would be okay. I believed him because I wanted to, but in reality, we were going around in circles.

> It is important to observe yourself in the experiences you have, and not make it about the other person. You are responsible for your own happiness and it is up to you to pay attention to what makes YOU as an individual happy. If you are living outside of your truth you will not be happy. It has nothing to do with the other person.

> We believe what we want to believe if it fits with our desires. This often keeps us stuck in situations that are unhealthy. If the words we hear match our beliefs but do not match the actions being taken – confusion results. This is quickly followed by anger and sadness. Eventually we have to get real and open our mind to the truth instead of hanging onto the hope that the belief is the truth.

Our life became a series of daily phone calls to say hello when he was either on the way to some airport, between business meetings or, going to a business dinner. If our work schedules worked, we met up once a month. I felt managed, definitely held at a distance, excluded from special occasions and from important people in his life, including his family, friends and colleagues. It was as if I was the other woman in a love affair, his lover, actually his secret lover. I began to feel more and more empty, lonely and sad. When we were together we were a strong and loving couple, he made me laugh with his charm and unique sense of humour, but in truth we lived separate lives and this became very obvious.

> Until we trust ourselves enough to open our heart to another person, love is a game that we do but cannot trust or even truly feel. Love is the nourishment our heart desires but once we close down our heart pain is locked in and our mind kicks in as we try to protect our heart from more pain. This keeps us locked in the pain cycle. It requires immense courage and vulnerability to open our heart again once we have been hurt as ego has strengthened and works hard to resist taking these steps Sadly, it then becomes easier to avoid love altogether.

We continued to talk about it, but nothing changed. The truth was he was happy as things were and as long as I was willing to settle for this, as he said, we would be ok. With never any true intention from him to extend his life from the one he had organised into little boxes that never interconnected and he determinedly controlled with meticulous detail and military precision - it appeared to be of paramount importance for him to have everything separate and he was prepared to do anything to make sure things stayed that way.

I am the opposite. I am open with my own life and never have been able to be kept in a mental/emotional box – therefore, this was a major problem for me. **I came to the conclusion that whatever was happening in his other life, and believe me, I considered every possibility, became completely irrelevant. The important point being, I was not part of it. To continue** on, knowing I was being intentionally excluded, was grossly disrespectful to me, period. In addition, continuing to listen to the reasons, excuses and justifications, would be participating and playing the unconscious game of enabling the fear that drove it to be sustained. At the same time, what was more important, I would consistently be sending a subtle but powerful message to my subconscious that I was not good enough and indirectly abusing MYSELF.

> What we accept for ourselves is our internal self-love and value barometer.

Chapter 4
Crossing the Crossroad

Now fully recognising this reality, I was at a crossroad. My self-worth had reached the tipping point where I could no longer stay in any situation settling for less than I deserved, or be treated with anything less than deep respect, honour and value – even if it was unintentional! This did not come from a place of ego, but from compassion and kindness for myself. In all of my relationships I had constantly doubted if I was good enough. Suddenly, as if a bolt of lightning had hit me in the heart, all my doubts, stories, questions and fears disappeared, I had become strong enough to ask the right questions, the hard questions and make clear decisions that sent the unmistakably powerfully loving message to myself - I AM ENOUGH! I was paying attention, listening and aware of how I was feeling in all the situations and conversations. When things made no sense, I asked for clarification. I absolutely loved him but now, for the first time, felt equal love for myself.

> The trouble with living with low self-esteem from childhood is that we do not believe we deserve anything really. We learn not to consider ourselves too much.

> Happiness is something other people enjoy. We settle into the fact that this is what life is all about: pain, struggle and sadness.

The final straw eventually came when I was evacuated from my house three times within a few weeks due to the river outside bursting its banks and the town being devastated by floods. During the second evacuation I texted him a picture of the sandbags and flooding water saying I was okay but it was happening again. I got a text message back saying "I'm out running errands, stay safe." That was the last I heard from him for three days. It was New Year time and he was not working but "busy." Was I angry, actually no, but I was empty. He called en-route home from his holidays sounding tired from the long haul journey and apologised for not calling during the flooding. I heard the excuses but I was still empty. The next day he called back after work. "How are you?" he asked. "I'm okay," I said, actually meaning it. He apologized again for not being in touch. "I tried to call," he said. "Yes," I agreed. "You could have made a bigger effort." "I couldn't get through because of the weather," he continued explaining. "I'm sorry I don't buy it, you have an iPhone, iPad, iWatch, landline phone, there was a way to get in touch but you didn't. The whole flooding thing is quite a big deal especially as I'm trying to sell my house and this is going to impact the sale." I was clear and matter-of-fact. He was due to come over in a couple of weeks' time and he turned the conversation to focus on that. "What are we doing with this relationship?" I continued to delve. "We can talk about it when I get there." "No, I need to talk about it now," I said adamantly. I was not going to fobbed off. "Do you see us together in the future?" "I don't know what I see in the future," he said completely deflecting the question. "Okay let me put it another way – do you want me in your future?" Finally I felt strong enough and had enough value for my life to ask him a direct question that was framed in a way that had no room for a vague or ambiguous answer. There was silence on the other end of the phone. Silence was my loud and clear answer. "You have nothing?" I asked "After sixteen years – you have nothing to say." More silence. "Really?" Now, a little surprised but not completely, however very unlike me, I felt pretty unemotional. It seemed that my mouth was speaking in a completely detached way and my heart was being taken care of. "Your silence has said it all," I said suddenly peaceful. "Okay I can't believe I'm saying this but I have to let this go, I can't be in a relationship with no future it's unhealthy." More silence "Say something!" I said incredulously "I love you," he said, "Now I'm going to go." "Okay I love you too," and I laid the phone down. I knew that continuing to be in a relationship with no future was not an option I could consider. It would break my heart. There was no doubt in my heart that he was my soul man. I had allowed him into my heart completely, into all aspects of my life, but now in order to honour myself I had to let go. His silence spoke volumes and it was very clear that he was unable to fully open up and let me in.

We will not ask hard direct questions until we are ready to hear the answer. The 'right' question is often hard to ask, but until we do, we will talk in circles missing the point we are trying to make. The right questions cannot

> be misinterpreted and are not vague. They are about getting the clarity we need to make the decisions that are true for our heart, soul and overall happiness.

At last I had reached the stage of loving myself enough to truly accept where I was and consider what I needed. At the same time, I loved him enough to accept where he was and that he couldn't, wouldn't or did not want us to build a life together. Life is too short to waste time living in hope - wishing for the day we may never see, so I let go with absolute love, more certain than ever, that love is never the issue but fear of vulnerability, insecurity, protection and need always are!

> Vulnerability is the key to true intimacy.

Vulnerability, the key to true intimacy, was impossible: he couldn't, or wouldn't let me too close. His powerful mind was in control, protecting him and not allowing him to trust again. It was the saddest thing to witness.

> Paradoxically, when we are trying to protect ourselves from pain, we create more pain. When we are focused on the pain from our past, it locks the pain inside, and blocks love from growing in our own hearts preventing it from coming into our lives. Our hearts thrive in love not pain.

My dear friend and insightful spiritual mother had once told me I was to show this man how to love again and I did to the best of my abilities. **But love has to come from within each one of us.** My unconditional love for him would never be enough until he was able to open his own heart, let out the hurt and receive that love.

Unconditional love comes with acceptance of the reality as it is, that is accepting the people in reality as they are including yourself. Unconditional love of yourself is crucial before you can have unconditional love of another person, loving them enough to let them go, loving yourself enough to accept you deserve to have what you want and not settle for less than that.

You get what you settle for. This is ideal if you are happy, but if it's less than what you need, want, deserve or are ready for - it is all you will get. To create the space to allow what we want to come into our lives, we must let go of our fear of losing to open up to attract what we deserve. Many people are not prepared to let go of what they have, even though it may not be working for them. It may even be abusive, but because they are afraid they will end up with nothing if they hang on to old situations that are unfulfilling. The other component is *WE MUST KNOW WHAT WE WANT, AND TRULY BELIEVE WE DESERVE IT.*

My loyalty and commitment to him was without doubt, but until then, I lacked loyalty to myself. Still, as deeply in love as I was from the beginning, I would have done anything for him and that was the problem - for a long time I loved him far more than I loved myself, but now there was a radical change. He never had any real intention of moving our relationship forward. It seemed his past pain was still calling the shots in his life, and sadly he believed it couldn't be healed, so he managed it instead. My philosophy and experience is the total opposite: **I believe with willingness and openness. In small**

baby steps we can all begin to heal, if not we become victims of our childhood or old painful relationships. In my opinion this is not necessary, but we do need to be ready to open and let go of the old story that feeds the false ego self and becomes our identity.

> Joining the dots to see the bigger picture happens when we are ready to see it. The more healed and whole we become, the stronger our inner strength is and we are able to handle more. The more fear we have, the smaller and narrower our view of life becomes. We can only see small segments of the whole and this keeps us in illusion and then we can make up the rest of the picture to fit with our dreams and desires rather than look at the reality as it truly is.

Back to our meeting all those years ago, with my fragile and low self-esteem and basic conceptual understanding of spirituality and consciousness, locked into a vicious cyclic illusion of fear and insecurity: I was lost, living an unconscious existence with unhealthy thoughts and habits. Pain and anxiety fueled all my decisions and actions. I felt like the luckiest of lucky to meet a person who, in my mind without doubt was my soul mate, a mirror reflecting my own possibilities.

My belief then was that meeting a soul-mate meant that we would be together for the rest of our lives. Now I know better and have a different belief, and understand our meeting was an opportunity for us both to heal something within.

> Our beliefs change as we develop and get older and wiser. Beliefs feel true but are not the truth or even

facts: they are just beliefs. They are not wrong, but they simply change when we grow in awareness.

Thankfully I took the opportunity and awakened further to increase my own life potential. Our meeting was an acceleration of the awakening that had already begun. He accepted me when I did not accept myself, wanted nothing from me when I was a chronic giver, encouraged me to believe in myself when I did not. This gave me the confidence to step out of my comfort zone and change my life completely. It was a game changer! Now I understood the meaning of love without need and for this, the gratitude from deep within my soul is endless. I regard myself to be very fortunate, to have healed so much from my past and had the ability to be open and vulnerable enough to do so. Not everyone is able to go there.

Stepping outside and expanding our comfort zones is the way to building confidence, self-esteem and becoming fearless.

Do I miss him? Yes! Do I love him? Absolutely! Do I need him to make me happy? No! Not at all! In truth I am happier now, out of the situation, - why? Because being in a loving relationship with anyone who is physically and emotionally unavailable is one of the saddest and loneliest places in the world to be.

Leaving any situation we know is creating sadness for us instantly makes us happier.

As I look back on that whole situation, I see it was an incredible opportunity to wake up and make the life changes that I desperately needed. For this I have an immense gratitude.

It completely changed my life and I am a happier, stronger person as a result. But the journey is life-long, a never-ending wonderful and crazy, bumpy ride and one that is not over yet. Thankfully, there's still more to come!

If the connection to ourselves is weak or broken, or the relationship is unhealthy because our unconscious habits and lack of awareness, re-enforces low self-worth or even in some instances self-hatred, where we have no value, compassion or love for ourselves, then we will desperately search for love from others making them the answer to our happiness. This dynamic brings immense pressure and need into the relationship, and we begin to play the game of co-dependency, which can eventually erode the love that we feel we have at the beginning. When we have built a healthy loving relationship with ourselves, where we are listening and honouring ourselves, we then share this with another who has done the same. Then we will have a completely different type of relationship that is not needy and co-dependent, but loving, kind and respectful.

The amazing rollercoaster of experiences continues and the journey never ceases to amaze me. I paused my life to write the story of my own journey and to find my way through the eternal cycles of unconscious Neverland. Each step through the minefield of the sometimes but not always painful experiences was taken with a decision to find my inner strength. By reaching out and asking for help when necessary, I learned how the power of vulnerability strengthens love and brings more wisdom. I count my many, many, blessings with gratitude and thanks to the powers that be, for the opportunities, people, gifts and importantly the many challenges that were part of this amazing road. Taking a breath in the stillness of the moment, feeling balance and peace once more in my life, I look forward to the next chapter of my story. There is limitless sunshine still to come…

Chapter 5
To You, For You

Loving yourself. What does this really truly mean? We know how important it is, with many books, videos, seminars and workshops available on the topic. It's surrounding us, bombarding us with its importance the whole time. Conceptually we think we know what it is and those of us who explore it think we know how to bring it into our lives. Some of us have awakened enough to begin the unlearning process, to create new healthier behaviours from those we were taught, but how many of us reach a level of self-love and awareness needed, to stop passing on old pain and from being hurt over and over again?

My awakening came in stages. Each time my life was in ruins, when I lost everything, or was broken mentally, emotionally, physically and spiritually, it became an opportunity every time I came through the other side, to experience compassion and consciousness awareness deeper than I had known before. In my early years as a child, teenager, young adult, self-love was not an option I was even aware of, far less something I practised. I lived in major denial. By working and making connections, life as I knew it was over, and I became a person who understood love and consciousness. A person who could feel, who was healing and who lived instead of existing and who grew emotionally and spiritually.

> Self-awareness is a never-ending, life long process. There are limitless levels of conscious awareness available to us and as we deepen our awareness, we can go through many challenging, sometimes painful rites of passage. This brings the necessary vulnerability and humility, which helps us to strengthen our spiritual connection, and increases heart wisdom, compassion and love.

> Through digging into old conditioning, behaviours, beliefs and mindsets that limit and block us, we will see that we all deserve happiness, love and respect. But if we settle for what we have, and believe it's all there is, we will never have what we truly deserve.

My life now is about helping people who have had enough of pain, playing the games of denial and avoidance - those who are ready to wake up, who want to live and not just exist by going through the motions, those who want peace, freedom, health, wealth and happiness in their lives. Those who are ready for conscious balanced relationships that honour, respect, and lovingly nourish everyone involved.

> It begins with YOU....

> In all the situations that you are in, or have ever been involved with, you are a common denominator, and are playing a role. Whether you perceive the situations as good, bad, right or wrong, you were in them. How

you see them and how you react to these experiences depends on how awake you are at the time. Life has a way of offering all sorts of opportunities and circumstances to help us wake up, learn and grow. Often these situations are not easy to go through, but we will not grow from them if we get stuck blaming this and that on something or someone else. As we can grasp this, we begin to halt the perpetuation of our victim story, and gain strength and empowerment from each situation rather than allowing it to weaken or disempower us. It is a choice.

How can we deepen our self-awareness?

Firstly we have to begin to know ourselves, and begin the challenging inner journey. Initially we often have great resistance to look inwards at ourselves. Ego shows up and tells us the problems we are having are because of other people, and easily points the finger away from us as part of the problem. Getting past this crucial step can be difficult but with an open mind and a little humility, our heart will expand and love will grow. It's often the case that pain is the component to begin our inner search.

We send unconscious messages to ourselves the whole time and those messages will be reflected back to us from the outside world to help us to see and learn something about ourselves. If the message we send to ourselves over and over again is "You don't matter," or "I'll get to you eventually but other people's needs are more important" you re-enforce low self-esteem, lack of value and increase victim and martyr consciousness. This eventually builds resentments and we will be taken more and more for granted. This disturbing belief that our needs and happiness aren't important, and that we matter less than other people is extremely self-destructive. This is ego. We all matter, and with awareness, the message we can choose to send ourselves is this: We all matter!

So now you know the Why are you ready to begin? What now? How does it work?

The fact is, we live extremely busy lives these days: we are constantly on the go with never ending drive, striving to say and do more and more of the right thing, or the current trend of the right thing. We are under pressure to be constantly juggling work, family, and social lives. The balance of our lives can easily be knocked out as we run around to the demands of busier and busier lifestyles. It becomes more and more difficult for us to self-love.

So we do self-love, or what think it is, spending an hour or two at the gym, practising yoga or meditating, convincing ourselves we are on it, trying to bring balance into our day.

Meanwhile the other 22-23 hours a day are spent running around like headless chickens. We over commit, over do, over-give, and are under pressure and are over stimulated. During sleep, our minds are often still whirling around unable to stop, mentally caught in the loop of fight or flight as our sympathetic nervous system locks us into a perpetual cycle of busyness. This becomes our norm until eventually we crash and burn or get sick. In that moment we cry, "What happened? I don't understand. I take care of myself. I love myself, I practise yoga. I meditate and exercise."

Yes, all true, but we have probably justified our over-stimulated, over-worked, out-of-balance lives, ignoring reality. This, along with our inability to really listen to what we truly need in the moment gives us the illusion that we look after ourselves. Self-care has been added to the drive, that our lives have become. To convince ourselves that we are taking care of ourselves we talk to everyone about how we do it, posting messages on social media, our egos desperately needing to prove to ourselves, and everyone, that we are on it. Sound familiar? We have normalised ourselves to over-living, over-doing, over-committing to others, often taking no time to listen, connect, or hear what we need, far less take the action steps to become loving, kind, and compassionate with ourselves. Our unconscious habits of quickly beating up on ourselves at the drop of a hat and giving ourselves a hard time continues, when we feel we haven't done something or ANYTHING well enough. This keeps us in a low vibration of self-abuse and pain. We easily become our own worst enemies as we hide behind our heavily disguised, but well-intentioned doing of self-love.

Here is a simple 5 Step process towards truly being in charge of building self-love. Use this as a daily practice and as a tool when necessary and feel the difference.

1. STOP

- *To even be in the position of being able to love ourselves we first of all need to **STOP**. Most of the time we are furiously racing through our lives,*

*never stopping long enough to listen to what we
need at any one moment.*

- *We jump out of bed hurry, through breakfast,
(if we have it at all) rush to work, often driving
through heavy traffic, skip lunch or eat on-the-go.
We are in the habit of saying yes to all the constant
demands and pressures before we take time to
think what we are doing, drink too much coffee,
tea and alcohol to keep ourselves going. Then there
are the demands of our social and family life.*

- *To convince ourselves that we are looking after
ourselves, we go to the gym, exercise or do yoga
for an hour or two, which of course helps, but if we
are afraid to miss the gym the choice is made from
fear not value. If we are lucky maybe we will meditate for a few minutes, all to prove to ourselves
we are balanced. For many of us, our point of
reference, or the ability to stop and check in with
where we are, has gone, if we even had it in the
first instance. It can be extremely uncomfortable
to stop for a few minutes to do nothing but listen
to our own hearts. Guilt-driven stories flow into
our minds, saying we are being lazy or irresponsible. This fear and guilt-driven belief keeps us
running and chasing our tails as we relentlessly
spin around the fast lane of our lives.*

- *Without ever stopping for long enough to even
begin to know how we feel, we talk about self-care,
from the conceptual or literal understanding of*

*how it looks, to stop and do nothing for a minute. This in itself is crazy as love is something we **feel** and not something we think.*

- *If we don't get into the habit of stopping for a minute to check in with ourselves, how can we truly know what we need for our own well-being at any time of the day or night?*

- *The first step to place us **into the position of being able to love ourselves** is to stop. Stopping is for taking a few deep breaths. A conscious inhale followed by a conscious exhale. Take a deep connected breath, then take another, then another, and continue to take slow conscious breaths until you feel the peace and calmness that connection brings. **This is essential before taking any action.***

- *The demands of life can scatter and fragment us, quite literally making us feel emotionally and energetically all over the place. We even say, "I'm shattered. I feel all over the place or I'm falling apart!" Breathing consciously helps to pull us back together.*

- *When we are all over the place it is difficult for us to make clear healthy choices that are best for our wellbeing. We react rather than respond. Build the habit of slowing down, using your breath when faced with any choice, big or small. Practising this habit places you into the position of truly bringing self-love into your life.*

2. STILL

- *Stillness is the next step required to take us towards self-love. How so? Because we can stop, but stopping does not mean that we are still, although it is necessary to stop before we can move into feeling still: that is, we have stillness of mind and body.*

- *Stillness comes with focus and practice. It is a state of centeredness and presence. Stillness is quietness, felt when our mind and body is at peace. Presence is being completely rooted in the present moment, mentally and emotionally.*

- *Stillness puts us into the position of being able to listen to what is true, right and healthy for us in that moment. It allows us to connect to our own truth on a deeper level. Any decisions that we make from a place of stillness are normally much clearer, healthier and conscious. Also they are usually less reactive and are likely to be more neutral and better for our wellbeing.*

These first two steps are vital to put us into the position to listen to our quiet inner voice. Without these steps we continue in the old habits of reactivity, jumping to conclusions, assumptions, people pleasing, and creating anxiety in our lives. The practice of stopping and becoming more still helps us to respond to choices in more conscious ways, therefore making decisions from awareness, value for our wellbeing, honesty, and respect for ourselves and others.

3. LISTEN

- *Listening is a crucial step to our self-care. The purpose of this step is to get to know who we are a little better: what we like, want or need. It helps us build more trust and respect for ourselves as we listen to ourselves as if we are our own best friend, one who is really interested in us.*

- *In my workshops, sometimes I ask participants, "What do YOU want?": The response is frequently a blank look as if they have been asked the most difficult question in the world. After a few moments a stunned expression comes over their face and they stumble and stutter, answering with another question: "Who me? What do I want?" "I don't know, I've never really thought about what I want, or have ever given that question any real consideration before." This response is very common and an indication of how far away from self-love some of us are. The unconscious habit of never really considering our own wants, needs, desires, hopes and dreams, on a moment-to-moment, day in day out basis prevents us from any ability to know or love ourselves. To listen is essential, and a necessary step, but there is an even deeper level of listening available. Initially, we listen by filtering everything through the ego mind, which can be sometimes tainted with unconscious thought processes.*

To truly listen from a place of compassion, kindness, and humbleness, is not the same as listening from our ego minds. We have to drop down to another level where we listen with our hearts. Listening from our ego mind, we are able to talk ourselves out of what is true for us, as fear, old conditioning and beliefs can still drive our decisions. Once we drop in to our hearts, we are now listening from a different place, feeling with our consciousness, our individual truth, from honour, love and respect for ourselves. Hearing without attachment our deeper truth.

4. HEAR

- *Hearing is not the same as listening. Hearing connects us to a deeper place within. It comes from our individual truth, our spirit and the wisdom of our soul. Listening comes from a necessary mental place, as it allows us to be in the position to hear. When we drop down to the deeper place and we hear rather than listen, we get a different answer, a clearer answer that feels peaceful, where there are no more questions, even if the answer we are hearing isn't palatable.*

- *Our individual truth always feels peaceful. Often what we hear doesn't make rational or logical sense but somehow we know without knowing why, that we have found our truth in that moment. We often find we are no longer concerned if others like, understand or are happy with what is right for us, of course we don't wish to harm or upset anyone – including ourselves. We just know it is right for us. If there is no judgment of ourselves, any judgment coming towards us from others will not penetrate, and has little or no affect on us at all. This is not the same as not caring for others. With our hearts open: of course we care for them, we simply no longer need their permission or approval. It's the closed pain-filled heart that selfishly does not truly care for anyone but himself or herself.*

5. ACTION

- *The action part is crucial to understand that as we go through these 5 steps and arrive on the action step, we are acting in response to a decision that we have made that is true, honest, respectful and right for us as individuals. We are not acting from fear or any need for permission or approval from anyone else. We are connected to our own truth and are simply honouring that truth and no longer re-acting habitually, mindlessly doing the same thing over and over. When we stop and breathe, positioning ourselves to becoming calm and still, listening, then as we drop deeper into our higher truth, hearing with our hearts, the actions that we take come from a more loving place, not only to ourselves, but to those around us that we also love.*

- *Action taken from this place is responding not reacting, it is responding to a choice, a decision* *made from value, honor and respect, one that we are making with no intention to harm, manipulate or control anyone or anything, a decision free from judgment or fear. We now have the **ability to respond** responsibility for the good of our wellbeing, value, self-care and self-love. It is responding from a place of respect for our lives. It builds the greatest power we can ever access, the power of true love, honor, compassion, kindness and strength.*

Listening then hearing on a deeper level is essential, but self-love is about balance. There are a number of habits that we have to unlearn as we become aware and move into more self-love. It is important to look at these old habitual habits that we can mindlessly continue and will keep us locked in drama, fear, insecurity, and ultimately pain.

When we are unlearning and letting go of any habit or old way of behaving, we must commit to reinforce over and over our new healthier habit with vigilance and mindfulness until it becomes our new normal. Otherwise, our old habit will show up again and instantly fill the space.

Strategies for Strengthen your Inner Power

When we are struggling with pain, self-esteem issues, depression, anxiety, loneliness or sadness, there are tools to use and a formula to follow that can change perspectives and bring concrete results. Working with these strategies as a daily practice and using them in times of stress and anxiety can change our direction from survival to living a life of more peace, freedom, fearlessness of judgment, confidence, inner strength and love.

Conscious Breathing

- *One of the first practices is to slow down the breath that moves through your body. Close your eyes and lie on a comfortable surface then place your hands on your navel one on top of the other, feel your belly rise and fall as you breathe deeply in an out of your belly. As you are doing this begin to repeat your name silently in your mind. This technique helps you to redirect your focus and connect to yourself a little more.*

- *Many people have a great deal of trouble saying their own name. This can be due to fragmentation and disconnection, usually caused by pain or trauma. Inhale and say your name then exhale and say your name. Practise this for a few minutes every morning and also before sleep, and as a tool in times of anxiety, to bring back a feeling of control of yourself. When practising this if you notice your mind beginning to wander onto something else, do not give yourself a hard time, but simply focus back to your name. With practice it gets easier.*

Complaining

- *Stop complaining about anything, everything or anyone. Do not complain verbally, silently in your mind, or with gossip, just simply stop, do not do it, period! It is a habit that feeds drama, negativity and pain and it will get you nowhere, except into a bigger hole. To clarify there is a difference between complaining and acknowledging something that is not working. It's important to acknowledge but it crosses the line into complaining if you start talking to everyone and anyone about the disaster, drama or event that has happened. Complaining feeds victim consciousness, and it will lock you into helplessness and disempowerment. This is a very unconscious and common habit and one that takes you further away from self-love. Acknowledge your problem then look for a solution – there is one. You can find it!*

Gratitude

- *Gratitude is the opposite of complaining, and an excellent way to help break down the complaining habit. Dig deep to find things to be grateful for, especially if your victim has taken hold. Starving your victim is hugely important to move closer to love and take care of yourself. Victim consciousness feeds on stories, dramas, and complaints. It is a form of ego with an energy that is stressed, needy and angry. Gratitude starves the victim consciousness. It is the completely opposite energy vibration. Gratitude genuinely felt in the heart is peaceful, soft, kind and full of love. Write down the things you are grateful for every day to build the energy of gratitude and abundance around you. What you focus on expands - Focus on what you have and it will grow!*

Acknowledge your Achievements

- *Any time you do anything that for you is a BIG DEAL, write it down. This can be anything unique to you, something that is not within your usual comfort zone, or that stretches you. Whatever it is, however small or insignificant it may feel to you, acknowledge it and write it down. Often we do things that for us are a big deal but to someone else it's nothing, no deal at all. Very simply, if something is a big deal for you, then **it is a big deal**, and deserves your acknowledgment. Recording them is a great way to build a book of evidence of your own growth. This is a fantastic tool that you can revisit in the days when you may not feel quite as strong. Your achievements matter!*

Comparing Yourself

- *Do not compare yourself to another unique person. It is an utter waste of time. If used, as it often is, to keep you feeling less than others, it is a type of self-abuse. You are a unique individual human being. There is nobody like you anywhere in the world. Think about your fingerprints, we all have them, but nobody has the same ones as anyone else, anywhere. Embrace and nurture your uniqueness. You matter!*

Voluntary Explaining

- *Offering explanations for everything that you do is a negative habit that will unconsciously lower self-worth and self-esteem. It is feeding a need for approval. It re-enforces our belief that we are not good enough, and our fear of upsetting or causing a reaction from other people, needing them to be ok with what we are doing. If they do not agree with us, are unhappy, or do not give us the approval we need, the people pleaser in us may force us to change what is right for us and go with what they want instead. Our need for approval opens us to being manipulated and in turn we become manipulators. As we grow in awareness and give ourselves the self-value that we deserve, the need for permission, or approval from other people, becomes less important to you. You are enough and your life matters!*

The I'm Sorry Habit

- *Being in the habit of apologising for every little thing sends a frequent message to yourself that you have done something wrong, that you are responsible for things that go wrong even when it has nothing to do with you. It comes from fear and feeds guilt. Say sorry only when you have actually done something to be sorry for. Get out of the habit of apologising for being alive. You matter!*

Excuses

- *Excuses are reasons and justifications as to why we are not doing something that we have said we would, committed to, or are procrastinating about. Excuses put the brakes on moving forward with our lives. They are often coming from protection, fear, and sometimes are not even honest. Stop making excuses for yourself and listening to excuses from others. See them for what they are lies, smoke screens and illusions to stay stuck and to avoid commitment. A fact based on reality is not the same as an excuse. Excuses will stop you from growing and moving forward in your life. Let go of using excuses and grow, to live your life to the fullest – Your life matters!*

Decisions of Value

- *We make zillions of decisions every day. As people pleasers with low self-esteem we usually check in with everyone else first before making any decisions. The balance goes way off and we end up being at the low end, if not the bottom of the priority list. This sends us a message that we don't matter and increases low-value and self-esteem problems. To help build up your self-worth make at least five decisions daily where you place yourself at the top of the priority list, checking in with yourself before others some of the time, decisions where the priority is to honour yourself. When faced with a decision, ask yourself, is this honouring me or is this dishonouring me. Using honor as your internal self-love barometer is a very powerful way to develop internal compassion. At the beginning when you put yourself and your needs first, it is normal to feel guilty. Do it anyway! Honour yourself – you matter!*

Questions

- *Ask high-quality questions. Our brains are wired to find the answers to the questions we ask, it is therefore extremely important to ask high- quality questions such as "How can I show myself......? When fear is predominately in our minds and running our lives, at that particular moment, we are locked into relative unconsciousness, particularly on the emotional level. "What if" questions asked from a fear-based root create more fear and anxiety. The quality of those questions is poor, as a lot of the time there is either no real answer, or the answer has not landed yet. This causes extreme anxiety, and can block us from moving forward. Only use "What if?" questions rooted in the positive, to explore the incredible, limitless possibilities that exist to create your future success. When you decide you can – You can!*

Be Present

- *Our point of power is rooted in the present moment. That is, we are mentally present and our minds are not wandering into past situations that we no longer have any control over, or future possibilities or events that may or may not happen. We are also physically connected and focused and we are emotionally aware of how and what we are feeling. At the same time we are witnessing, without judgment what is around us in that precise moment. Focus on the present moment to strengthen your inner power!*

Exercise

- *Get your body moving daily, preferably in the fresh air. Your health matters!*

Guilt – the killer of joy

- *Guilt is a story that is rooted in fear, and drives many people to do, say and act in ways that they would prefer not to. We are often spoon-fed guilt and it is a tool used against us by others to manipulate, to get us to do what they want and usually serves them in some way. Used against us it feels terrible and creates a lot of stress, pain and anxiety, destroying self-esteem and self-worth. It has the power to make us live outside of our truth and that in turn causes depression. Used by us towards others, to get what we want, it initially feels powerful and we even feel clever, but this is normally short-lived and it often comes back to bite us. If you don't want guilt, don't use or swal-*

low it. Dump guilt stories and live from love – you matter!

Power of Vulnerability

- *Another way to see vulnerability is being emotionally honest in the moment. We are afraid to be vulnerable as it may appear weak or possibly our vulnerability has been exploited by unconscious people in the past. Being vulnerable is important in our healing process, and is essential to achieve intimacy and connection. But it also extremely important to use wisdom and be wise with whom you are open and vulnerable as it can and will be exploited by the unconscious people who are around, some of them heavily disguised. Heal old emotional heart pain wisely and safely by opening up to your honest vulnerability with a trusted person – healing your heart matters!*

Take Time for yourself

- *Taking time and space for yourself is essential. You will rarely be given time – you have to be the one to take it. It is not selfish it is taking care of your self to nourish your soul.*

Meditate

- *Daily meditation helps you gain clarity, focus, energy, balance, and gives you the opportunity to bring peace and stillness into todays busy, demanding overwhelming fast-paced crazy life.*

We are creators of our own realities, and because what we create starts with a thought, or an idea, it is therefore important to use the immense power of our minds wisely, ensuring that we look after our thoughts and not allow fear and drama to clutter our minds. When we focus on negativity, pain and fear we create more of the same, but on the other hand and just as potently, we can create the entire opposite of this by focusing on a different perspective. It is a choice, but one that only comes with awakening and consciousness to the other possibilities that exist in our lives. We can settle for what we have been given, including any of the old limiting beliefs and mindsets that have been passed on to us, or, if we want to, with openness, humility, vulnerability and commitment we can change them, especially if the beliefs and mindsets are not supporting our happiness, to live a life of love and compassion. You choose.

Letter to the reader

Dear Reader,

Thank you so much for taking the time to read my book. I sincerely hope that you enjoyed reading it and gained some insight and strength from the experience.

If you did enjoy reading this book and feel that others would also benefit, I would be very grateful if you would send a review to amazon to encourage others to buy.

If you have any questions from reading "Sunshine in Neverland" or are interested in more information on seminars and healing workshops or private sessions please feel free the contact me at

info@moiradarling.com or at

www.moiradarling.com

With so much gratitude and kindness for your future

Moira Darling

About the Author

Scottish born Moira Darling has been teaching and empowering people worldwide since her transformational awakening seventeen years ago. Her unique down-to-earth, common sense approach to spirituality and empowerment along with a natural intuitive gift and ability to translate and clarify energies, has changed the lives of thousands of people over the years. Moira has returned to her Scottish roots but travels extensively bringing her profoundly, straightforward no nonsense clarity to the world. This is Moira's first book and is the story of her own transformational process that anyone who reads cannot fail to identify with and learn from.

Lightning Source UK Ltd.
Milton Keynes UK
UKOW06f1606050916

282241UK00011B/375/P